HOW TO READ A FINANCIAL REPORT

W9-AAA-939

HOW TO READ A

WRINGING CASH FLOW AND OTHER

Third Edition

WILEY

JOHN WILEY & SONS

NEW YORK · CHICHESTER · BRISBANE

FINANCIAL REPORT

VITAL SIGNS OUT OF THE NUMBERS

JOHN A. TRACY, Ph.D., CPA

TORONTO SINGAPORE

Copyright © 1989 by John Wiley & Sons, Inc.

All rights reserved. Published simultaneously in Canada.

Reproduction or translation of any part of this work
beyond that permitted by Section 107 or 108 of the
1976 United States Copyright Act without the permission
of the copyright owner is unlawful. Requests for
permission or further information should be addressed to
the Permissions Department, John Wiley & Sons, Inc.

This publication is designed to provide accurate and
authoritative information in regard to the subject
matter covered. It is sold with the understanding that
the publisher is not engaged in rendering legal, accounting,
or other professional service. If legal advice or other
expert assistance is required, the services of a competent
professional person should be sought. *From a Declaration
of Principles jointly adopted by a Committee of the
American Bar Association and a Committee of Publishers.*

Library of Congress Cataloging in Publication Data

Tracy, John A.
How to read a financial report: wringing cash flow and other
vital signs out of the numbers/John A. Tracy. — 3rd ed.
p. cm.
Bibliography: p.
Includes index.
ISBN 0-471-50745-8. — ISBN 0-471-50746-6 (pbk.)
1. Financial statements. I. Title.
HF5681.B2T733   1989
657'.3 — dc20   89-8962
                                                    CIP

Printed in the United States of America

10 9 8 7 6 5 4 3

PREFACE

Since the second edition was published in 1983, three major events have made a new edition necessary:

- ◆ Congress passed the Tax Reform Act of 1986, which changed depreciation methods, tax rates, and other topics discussed in this book
- ◆ The Financial Accounting Standards Board (FASB) mandated that a Cash Flows Statement must be included in financial reports
- ◆ The Auditing Standards Board made radical changes in the CPA auditor's report, which financial statement users should understand.

The third edition reflects these changes. Also, I have replaced the final chapter with an entirely new one, which should be much more interesting to securities investors.

I thank my publisher for the opportunity to update and polish the book. Making it to a third edition is very satisfying. It is especially gratifying to see that the book's cash flow emphasis has now been confirmed by the Financial Accounting Standards Board.

The professionals at John Wiley & Sons were very helpful again with this edition. I deeply appreciate the kind reviews of the previous editions, especially the review of the first edition by Todd Fandell in the *Chicago Tribune*. Thank you, Mr. Fandell.

It hardly seems possible that I wrote the preface to the first edition almost ten years ago. Reflecting on this decade I've come to realize more fully how indebted I am to my original editor, Gordon Laing. He deserves a major part of the credit for the book's success. Thanks very much, Gordon.

JOHN A. TRACY

Boulder, Colorado
July 1989

PREFACE TO THE FIRST EDITION

Are you a business manager who needs a better understanding of the financial reports of your own company? Are you a banker or investor who wants better insight into the financial statements of other companies? Do you have doubts about the meaning of some items in financial reports? Are you not sure what to look for?

This book is for you.

You have an interest in financial reports, but neither the time nor the need for an in-depth knowledge of accounting. Therefore, this book contains no discussions of bookkeeping procedure, data processing, or maintaining accounting records. Just as you might explain football to a friend attending a game for the first time, this book tells you the "rules of the game"—the *basic* accounting rules—how those numbers in the financial statements were arrived at, and what they really mean.

Behind all the numbers is a simple, vital concept you must never lose sight of—*cash flow*. Business is run by keeping money moving. Financial statements report *where the money came from, where it's invested for the time being*, and, most important, *how often it has turned over*. Learning to gauge cash flow is one of the most important rewards you will get from this book.

Newspaper readers are accustomed to a quick read. Users of financial statements, in contrast, must settle for a slow read. They have to know which messages to look for and which comparisons to make to get the messages. This book will teach you to read a financial report step by step. I've kept the number of steps to a minimum, and I make no unnecessary technical detours.

A word on accounting jargon: mastering a bit of accounting terminology is unavoidable if you want to understand financial statements. When a term is first introduced, it is carefully explained. But the way you master it is through repeated use. If at first you don't fully grasp a term, don't worry. Its meaning will become clear as we move along. By the end of the book you should have a good working knowledge of the language of accountants.

You'll look at a financial report with new awareness and new confidence in your ability to "unlock" the vital information it contains.

JOHN A. TRACY

Boulder, Colorado
October 1979

PREFACE TO THE SECOND EDITION

I'm tempted to take all the credit for the success of the first edition. To be honest, however, I had superb editors and the publisher produced a handsome book. So my thanks go to John Wiley & Sons, and deepest appreciation to Gordon Laing and Richard Lynch. I could ask for no better editors. Also, I'm most grateful for the many favorable reviews of the first edition, from the *Chicago Tribune* to *The Accounting Review*.

You may ask therefore: If the first edition has been such a good seller, why revise it? Recent developments in financial reporting, combined with the 1981 and 1982 changes in the income tax law, demand an updating of the book. This updating also provides the opportunity to make several improvements based on readers' comments and my experience in working with the book.

Most reviewers particularly like the centerpiece diagram in the first edition—the Master Exhibit that highlights the key connections among the basic financial statements. These cause-and-effect relationships are marked like highways on a roadmap. In this second edition the Master Exhibit has been extended to also show cash flow causes and effects. The name of the game today in business is cash flow, that's for sure.

JOHN A. TRACY

Boulder, Colorado
June 1983

CONTENTS

1

STARTING WITH CASH FLOWS

Importance of Cash Flows:
A Cash Flow Summary for the Business

Business managers, lenders, and investors are, quite rightly, very concerned with cash flows. Cash inflows and outflows are the heartbeat of any business. So let's start here. For our example we'll use a middle-size business that has just completed its first year of operations. The first year of business provides a fresh start, free of carry-over problems from previous years.

A summary of the company's cash receipts and cash disbursements for the first year of business is given in Exhibit A. Exhibit A shows three sources of cash receipts and five uses (disbursements) of cash during the year. Each source and use should be fairly familiar, so the following description of the company's activities is very brief:

♦ The company received money from the sale of products to its customers. Also, the company borrowed money on interest-bearing notes, and stockholders invested money in the corporation.

♦ The company paid out money for the purchase of products sold to its customers, and also paid out money for operating expenses, as well as for interest and income tax expenses. The company bought and paid for land, a building, machines and equipment, as well as office furniture.

EXHIBIT A—SUMMARY OF CASH RECEIPTS AND DISBURSEMENTS DURING FIRST YEAR

CASH RECEIPTS

From customers for products sold to them	$3,807,000	
From stockholders for which stock shares were issued	766,030	
From borrowing on interest-bearing notes payable	825,000	
Total cash receipts during year		$5,398,030

CASH DISBURSEMENTS

For purchases of products that were sold or are being held for sale	$3,162,000	
For many different expenses of operating the business	913,680	
For interest on notes payable	68,750	
For income tax based on taxable income of year	91,800	
For land, building, machinery, equipment, and furniture purchased at start of year, which will last several years	918,800	
Total cash disbursements during year		5,155,030
Increase in Cash during year, which is balance of Cash at end of year		$ 243,000

What Does the Summary of Cash Flows NOT Tell You?

What does Exhibit A tell you? One thing it tells you is that cash, that all-important lubricant of business activity, increased $243,000 during the year. Receipts exceeded disbursements by this amount for the entire year.

But, what does Exhibit A *not* tell you that you absolutely need to know? The two most important things that the cash summary does not tell you are:

1. The *profit* for the year.

2. The *financial condition* or position of the business at the end of the year.

Why doesn't Exhibit A tell you the profit earned during the year? Profit is the total revenue (gross proceeds) from sale of products to customers less all expenses of making the sales and operating the business. You can't count money borrowed or money invested by stockholders as sales revenue. Certainly you don't earn profit by borrowing money that has to be repaid later, or by stockholders investing capital in the business.

So the first step is to distinguish between two quite different sources of cash: (a) the cash received from sales revenue, and (b) the cash received from borrowing and stockholders' investments.

Next, we have to ask whether all the cash disbursements during the year are for expenses that should be deducted from sales revenue to determine profit. The first four disbursements in Exhibit A are certainly expense related. But the fifth disbursement is far too much to charge off entirely against sales revenue for the first year. These expenditures for land, a building, machines, equipment, and furniture are *long-term* investments. These resources are used over several years. To deduct all their cost in the year of purchase would be very misleading for profit measurement.

Two Basic Types of Cash Flows

At this point, therefore, we should divide the cash flows into the two groups shown below. This reveals that the company raised $1,591,030 capital from borrowing and stockholders, and invested $918,800 in certain long-term assets, leaving $672,230 cash available for other needs.

We have already seen that the ending cash balance is $243,000.

What happened to the difference of $429,230 ($672,230 less $243,000 = $429,230)? The business had negative cash flow from its profit-making operations for the year, as shown below. Is this the amount of *loss* for the year? Did the business suffer over $400,000 in loss for its first year? No, cash flows are not the whole story.

(1)
Cash Flows of Raising and Investing Capital

Received from borrowing	$ 825,000
Received from stockholders	766,030
Total	$1,591,030
Spent for long-term assets	918,800
Net increase of cash	$ 672,230

(2)
Cash Flows of Profit-Making Operations

Received from sales		$3,807,000
Spent for expenses:		
Purchases of Products	$3,162,000	
Operating Expenses	913,680	
Interest Expense	68,750	
Income Tax Expense	91,800	4,236,230
Net decrease of cash		$ 429,230

Profit Cannot Be Measured by Cash Flows

Hardly ever are cash flows during a certain period the correct amounts to measure profit (or loss) for that period. To start with, this company, like the vast majority of businesses, sells its products *on credit*. At the end of the year, this company has *receivables* from sales made to its customers during the last part of the year. These receivables will be collected (in cash) during the early part of the next year.

So the cash received during the year from customers is not total sales revenue for the year. The amount of receivables at year-end has to be added to the cash received. The *correct* sales revenue for the year is the sum of the two.

Cash disbursements are *not* the correct amounts for measuring expenses. Like sales revenue, the cash amount is not the whole story. The company paid out $3,162,000 for purchases of products during the year (see Exhibit A). At year-end, however, many products are still on hand in *inventory*. In other words, some of the products bought during the year have not yet been sold by the end of the year. Only the cost of products sold and delivered to customers during the year should be deducted as expense from sales revenue to measure profit.

Furthermore, some of its year-end inventory had not yet been paid for at year-end. The company buys its products on credit, and takes some time before paying its bills. So the company has a *liability* at year-end for these recent purchases.

The cash payments during the year for operating expenses, as well as for interest and income tax expenses, are *not* the correct amounts to deduct from sales revenue to measure profit for the year. The company also has *liabilities* at the end of the year for these expenses. The cash disbursement amounts shown in Exhibit A do not include the additional amounts of these expenses that are unpaid at the end of the year.

The main point is this: Cash flows are *not* the correct amounts needed to determine profit for a period of time. Cash flows do not include the complete sales revenue and expense activities for the period. A complete accounting is necessary to measure profit.

This "complete accounting" is known as the *accrual basis*. Accrual basis accounting records the receivables from making sales on credit, and also records the liabilities for unpaid expenses, in order to determine the correct profit measure for the period.

Accrual basis accounting is also necessary to get a complete look at the company's assets other than cash, as well as its liabilities and other sources of capital.

Cash Flows Do Not Reveal Financial Condition

The cash receipts and disbursements summary for the year (Exhibit A) does not reveal the financial condition of the company. The business manager certainly needs to know the asset situation of the company, that is, how much receivables, inventory, and other assets the company has. Also, the manager needs to know the amounts of the company's liabilities. The manager has the responsibility of keeping the company in a position to pay its liabilities when they come due. And the manager has to know whether the assets are too large (or too small) relative to the sales volume of the company. Lenders and investors are also very interested in the same things.

In short, managers, lenders, and investors all need a summary report of the financial condition (assets, liabilities, etc.) of a business. And they need a correct profit performance report, which sums up sales revenue and expenses for the year. A cash flow summary is also very helpful, but in no sense does it take the place of the other two reports. The next chapter introduces these two basic accounting reports.

2

INTRODUCING THE BALANCE SHEET AND INCOME STATEMENT

Managers, creditors, and investors need an accounting report that summarizes the present financial condition of the business. And they need a summary report that presents the correct sales revenue and expenses for the period just ended, to know the correct profit for the period. A cash flow statement, though very useful in its own right, does not provide the information needed concerning financial condition and profit performance.

Financial condition is presented in a report called the *Balance Sheet*. The profit performance summary is called the *Income*

Statement. Both are called financial statements, or just "financials." Alternative titles for the Balance Sheet include the *Statement of Financial Condition* and the *Statement of Financial Position*. Likewise, the Income Statement may be called the *Earnings Statement* or the *Statement of Operations*. An older term, not used as often today, is the *Profit & Loss Statement*. Minor variations on all these titles are common.

Exhibit B presents the Balance Sheet and Exhibit C presents the Income Statement of the same company whose cash flows

EXHIBIT B—BALANCE SHEET AT END OF FIRST YEAR OF BUSINESS

Current Assets			Current Liabilities		
Cash		$ 243,000	Accounts Payable		$ 269,120
Accounts Receivable		405,000	Accrued Expenses		130,390
Inventory		632,400	Income Tax Payable		10,200
Prepaid Expenses		77,760	Short-Term Notes Payable		300,000
Total Current Assets		$1,358,160	Total Current Liabilities		$ 709,710
			Long-Term Notes Payable		525,000
Property, Plant & Equipment					
Land, Building, Machines,					
Equipment, and Furniture	$918,800		**Stockholders' Equity**		
Accumulated Depreciation	(78,220)	840,580	Capital Stock	$766,030	
			Retained Earnings	198,000	964,030
Total Assets		$2,198,740	Total Liabilities & Stockholders' Equity		$2,198,740

are shown in Exhibit A. The form and content of the Balance Sheet and Income Statement apply to a very broad range of manufacturers, wholesalers, and retailers. These financial statements are quite typical for any business that buys or makes products that are then sold to their customers. In other words, the two accounting reports summarize the financial condition and profit-making activity of a company that deals in products.

EXHIBIT C—INCOME STATEMENT FOR FIRST YEAR

Sales Revenue		$4,212,000
Cost of Goods Sold Expense		2,740,400
Gross Margin		$1,471,600
Operating Expenses	$1,010,880	
Depreciation Expense	78,220	1,089,100
Operating Earnings		$ 382,500
Interest Expense		82,500
Earnings Before Income Tax		$ 300,000
Income Tax Expense		102,000
Net Income		$ 198,000

The financial statements you see in Exhibits B and C are for a company that has just completed its first year of business. The first year is a good place to begin the study of financial statements. For one thing, there is no carryover from previous years. Everything you see in the financial statements has happened this year; you don't have to refer back to previous years. The complete history of the company is reported in the financial statements.

Also, all the dollar amounts reported in this company's two financial statements are fairly recent values. Thus we avoid problems caused by "old" amounts that are included in the financial statements of a company that has been in business several years. We'll get to these problems later in the book.

In addition to the Balance Sheet and Income Statement a business also reports a third financial statement—the *Cash Flow Statement*, which summarizes cash inflows and outflows for the year. The cash flows of the company in our example have already been presented in Chapter 1. The format of this third financial statement and its connections with the other two main financial statements will be explained later, after we've gone through the Balance Sheet and Income Statement.

Income Statement

The Income Statement summarizes sales revenue and expenses over a period of time—for one year in Exhibit C. All the dollar amounts reported in this financial statement are cumulative totals for the period. The top line is gross proceeds, or total revenue from sales to customers. The bottom line is *net income* (also called net earnings), which is the final profit remaining after *all* expenses are deducted from sales revenue.

The Income Statement is designed to be read in a step-down manner, like walking down stairs. Each step down is a deduction of one or more expenses. The first step deducts the cost of goods (products) sold from the revenue from the goods sold, which gives the line called *gross margin* (sometimes called gross profit). This measure of profit is called "gross" because several other expenses are not yet deducted.

Next, operating expenses and depreciation expense are deducted, giving *operating earnings* before the interest and income tax expenses. Deducting interest expense from operating earnings gives *earnings before income tax*. Subtracting income tax expense from this gives the final step down to *net income*.

The Income Statement shown in Exhibit C reports four profit lines—gross margin, operating earnings, earnings before tax, and, finally, net income. However, some companies report only two profit lines. They add together all expenses below the gross margin line into one total amount, which is subtracted from gross margin to go directly to net income. There's no standard rule; reporting practices differ. The four line format in Exhibit C is useful in the following discussion.

The final bottom line profit measure in the Income Statement is simply sales revenue less all expenses. Is it true and accurate? This depends on whether sales revenue is measured correctly for the period *and* whether every expense is measured correctly for the period. These basic accounting measurement rules are discussed briefly at this point:

Sales Revenue—total amount received or to be received later from customers from the sales of products and services during the period. Sales revenue is net of (excludes) the following: discounts off list prices, prompt payment discounts, sales returns, and any other allowances or deductions from the original sales prices. Sales taxes are not included in Sales Revenue, nor are excise taxes that might apply.

Cost of Goods Sold Expense—total cost of the goods sold to customers during the period. Also, the cost of goods that were not sold but were shoplifted, stolen, or are otherwise missing, as well as write-offs and write-downs due to damage or obsolescence, are included in the Cost of Goods Sold Expense for the year. So this expense usually includes an extra charge for goods that did not produce any sales revenue during the period.

Operating Expenses—broadly speaking, every expense other than Cost of Goods Sold, Depreciation, Interest, and Income Tax. *Warning:* reporting practices for these expenses are not uniform. In Exhibit C only one total expense amount is reported for all operating expenses. But, in many cases, two or more may be reported. For example, marketing expenses may be separated from administration and general expenses, which is quite proper. Even in a relatively small business, there are hundreds of different operating expenses, some rather large and some very small. They range from salaries and wages of employees (large) to legal fees (preferably, small).

Depreciation Expense—fraction of the original cost of long-term operating assets (buildings, machinery, equipment, tools, furniture, and fixtures) that is recorded to expense during this period; this is the "charge" for using the assets during the period.

Interest Expense—total amount of interest on debt (interest-bearing liabilities) for the period. Other types of financing charges may also also be included, such as loan-fees.

Income Tax Expense—total amount due the government on the taxable income earned by the business during the period. This is determined by multiplying the taxable income for the period by the appropriate tax rates, less any credits (direct deductions). Income Tax Expense does not include other types of taxes, such as unemployment and social security taxes on payroll and property taxes, which are included in Operating Expenses. However, state income taxes are included.

Balance Sheet

The Balance Sheet format in Exhibit B follows fairly standardized and uniform rules of classification and ordering. (The Income Statement is somewhat more flexible.) Financial institutions, public utilities, railroads, and a few other rather specialized businesses use different Balance Sheet formats. But the large majority of industrial and retail businesses follow the Balance Sheet format shown in Exhibit B.

On the left side the Balance Sheet lists assets. On the right side it lists liabilities and owners' equity. The owners of a corporation are its stockholders. So, owners' equity is called stockholders' equity. Each separate asset, liability, and owners' equity reported in the Balance Sheet is called an *account*. Every account has a name (title) and a dollar amount, which is called its balance. For instance, from Exhibit B:

Name of Account	*Amount (Balance) of Account*
Inventory	$632,400

The other dollar amounts in the Balance Sheet are not accounts; they are subtotals or totals from adding (or subtracting) balances of accounts. A line is drawn to indicate that a subtotal or total is being taken.

The Balance Sheet is prepared at the close of business on the last day of the Income Statement period. If, for example, the Income Statement is for the year ending June 30, 1990, the Balance Sheet is prepared at midnight June 30, 1990. The accounts' balances reported in the Balance Sheet are the amounts at that precise moment in time. The financial situation of the business is "frozen" for one split second, as it were.

The Balance Sheet does not report the total flows into and out of the assets, liabilities, and owners' equity accounts during the period. Only the ending balance at the Balance Sheet date is reported for each account. For example, the company has an ending Cash balance of $243,000 (see Exhibit B). Can you tell the cash receipts and disbursements during the year? No, not from the Balance Sheet.

Balance Sheet accounts are subdivided into the following classes, or basic groups, in the following order of presentation:

Left Side	*Right Side*
(1) Current Assets	(1) Current Liabilities
(2) Property, Plant & Equipment	(2) Long-term Liabilities
(3) Other Assets	(3) Stockholders' Equity

Current Assets are cash and those other assets that will be converted into cash during one operating cycle. Assets not directly involved in the operating cycle (such as marketable securities or receivables from employees) are included in Current Assets if they will be converted into cash during the coming year.

The operating cycle refers to the sequence of acquiring products, holding the products until sale, selling the products, waiting to collect the receivables from the sales, and, finally, receiving the cash from the customers. This sequence is the most basic process of a business' operations; it's repeated over and over. The operating cycle may be short, only 60 days or less, or it may be relatively long, perhaps 180 days or more.

Although not as common today, in the past the assets grouped in the category Property, Plant & Equipment were called *Fixed Assets*. However, this term is not satisfactory. Fixed assets are not really fixed or permanent, excepting the land owned by a business. More accurately, these are long-term operating assets used by a business over several years, such as buildings, machinery and equipment, trucks, forklifts, office furniture, computers, and so on.

The cost of a long-lived operating asset, excepting land, is gradually charged off over its useful life. The cumulative amount of its cost that has been charged off since the date of acquisition up to the Balance Sheet date is in the Accumulated Depreciation account. The balance in this account is deducted from the original cost balance in the asset account.

Other Assets is a catchall class for the those assets that don't fit in either the Current Assets or Property, Plant & Equipment. The company in this example does not have any other assets.

The official definition of *Current Liabilities* runs 200 words, plus a long footnote. Briefly, these are short-term debts that for the most part depend on the conversion of current assets into cash for their payment. Also, other debts that will come due within one year from the Balance Sheet date are put in the Current Liabilities class. There are four accounts in this class—see Exhibit B again.

Long-Term Liabilities are debts whose maturity dates are more than one year after the Balance Sheet date. There's only one account in this class (see Exhibit B again). Either in the Balance Sheet or in a footnote to the statement, the maturity dates and other relevant provisions of all long-term liabilities should be disclosed. To simplify, no footnotes are presented here. Footnotes are discussed in Chapter 18.

Liabilities are claims on the assets of a business; cash or other assets that will be converted into cash later will be used to pay the liabilities. It's apparent, therefore, that liabilities should be accounted for in the Balance Sheet.

Liabilities are also *sources* of assets. Clearly, the total assets of a company increase when it borrows money. Also, a business has liabilities for unpaid expenses. The company has not had to use some of its assets to pay these liabilities.

The other reason for reporting liabilities in the Balance Sheet is to account for the sources of the company's assets—to answer the question: Where did the company's total assets come from? A complete Balance Sheet accounting requires that all sources of the company's assets be accounted for.

In addition to liabilities, the other basic source of a company's total assets is from its owners. The *Stockholders' Equity* class reveals the rest of the sources of a company's total assets. There are two basic stockholders' equity accounts—Capital Stock and Retained Earnings.

When the owners (the stockholders in the case of a corporation) invest capital in the business, the Capital Stock account is increased.* The amount of net income (profit) earned by a business less the amount distributed to its owners from the profit gives the amount of earnings retained in the business. This amount is recorded in the Retained Earnings account. The nature of Retained Earnings is confusing, and, therefore, is explained very carefully later in the book at the appropriate places.

* Many corporations issue par value stock shares; when they issue stock shares for more than par value the excess may be reported in a second stock account called Additional Paid-In Capital, or Paid-In Capital in Excess of Par Value. This is not shown in the example. This separation between the two accounts has little practical significance.

3

**PROFIT
ISN'T EVERYTHING**

The Threefold Task of Managers:
Profit, Financial Condition, and Cash Flow

The Income Statement reports the profit performance of the business. The ability of managers to make sales and to control expenses, and thereby to earn profit, is measured in the Income Statement. Clearly, earning an adequate profit is the key for survival and the manager's most important imperative. But the bottom line is not the end of the manager's task.

Managers must also control the *financial condition* of the business. This means keeping the assets and liabilities within proper limits and proportions relative to each other and relative to the sales and expense levels of the company. And, managers must *prevent cash shortages* that would cause the business to default on its liabilities or to miss its payroll.

The business manager really has a *threefold task:* earning profit, controlling the company's financial condition, and preventing "cashouts." Profit performance alone does not guarantee survival. In other words, you can't manage profit without also managing the changes in financial condition caused by the sales and expenses that produce your profit. Furthermore, the profit-making activity may actually put a temporary drain on cash rather than provide cash inflow.

The business manager should use the Income Statement to evaluate profit performance, and to ask a whole raft of profit-oriented questions. Did sales revenue meet the goals and objectives for the period? Why did sales revenue increase compared to last period? Which expenses increased more or less than they should have? And so on. These profit management questions are absolutely essential. But the manager can't stop at the end of these questions.

Beyond the profit analysis, the business manager has to move on to *financial condition* analysis and *cash flow* analysis. In large business organizations, responsibility for financial condition and cash flow usually is separated from profit responsibility. The vice-president of finance is responsible for financial condition and cash flow; other organization units are responsible for sales and costs. In these large companies the chief executive and the board of directors must oversee and approve the decisions of the financial vice-president. But most of the details can be and usually are delegated to the financial vice president of the corporation.

In middle-size and smaller businesses, however, the top-level manager or the owner/manager is directly and totally responsible for financial condition and cash flow. There's no one else to delegate these responsibilities to.

The Trouble with
Conventional Financial Statements

Unfortunately, the typical financial statements prepared by the accountant do not "pave the way" for financial condition and cash flow analyses. Conventional financial statements are not ready made for these purposes.

The Balance Sheet and Income Statement for a business, such as shown in Exhibits B and C, do not leave a clear trail of the "cross-over effects" between these two basic financial statements. The statements are presented on the assumption that the reader understands these couplings and linkages between the two statements and that the reader will make the appropriate connections and comparisons.

The Balance Sheet and Income Statement need to be accompanied by a cash flow statement. Only recently did the rule-making body of the accounting profession make the cash flow statement one of the *required* statements in financial reports. In the opinion of many, this change was long overdue. Managers, as well as creditors and investors, clearly need a cash flow statement that summarizes the major sources and uses of cash during the period.

Chapter 1 has already explained that cash flows are the natural center of gravity for business managers. Exhibit A (page 3) shows the cash flow summary for the company. To be most useful, however, the cash flow summary needs to be tied in with the company's Balance Sheet and Income Statement to understand the interlocking of all three statements.

EXHIBIT D—MASTER EXHIBIT

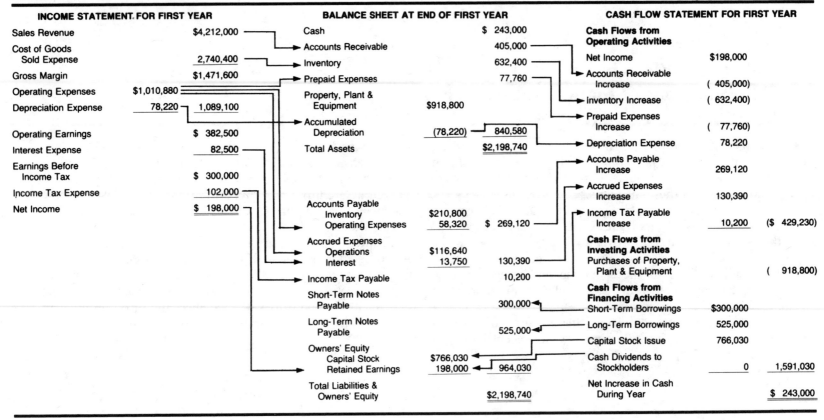

INCOME STATEMENT FOR FIRST YEAR			BALANCE SHEET AT END OF FIRST YEAR			CASH FLOW STATEMENT FOR FIRST YEAR		
Sales Revenue		$4,212,000	Cash		$ 243,000	**Cash Flows from Operating Activities**		
Cost of Goods Sold Expense		2,740,400	Accounts Receivable		405,000	Net Income	$198,000	
			Inventory		632,400			
Gross Margin		$1,471,600	Prepaid Expenses		77,760	Accounts Receivable Increase	(405,000)	
Operating Expenses	$1,010,880		Property, Plant & Equipment	$918,800		Inventory Increase	(632,400)	
Depreciation Expense	78,220	1,089,100	Accumulated Depreciation	(78,220)	840,580	Prepaid Expenses Increase	(77,760)	
Operating Earnings		$ 382,500				Depreciation Expense	78,220	
Interest Expense		82,500	Total Assets		$2,198,740	Accounts Payable Increase	269,120	
Earnings Before Income Tax		$ 300,000				Accrued Expenses Increase	130,390	
Income Tax Expense		102,000	Accounts Payable			Income Tax Payable Increase	10,200	($ 429,230)
			Inventory	$210,800				
Net Income		$ 198,000	Operating Expenses	58,320	$ 269,120			
			Accrued Expenses			**Cash Flows from Investing Activities**		
			Operations	$116,640		Purchases of Property, Plant & Equipment		(918,800)
			Interest	13,750	130,390			
			Income Tax Payable		10,200	**Cash Flows from Financing Activities**		
			Short-Term Notes Payable		300,000	Short-Term Borrowings	$300,000	
			Long-Term Notes Payable		525,000	Long-Term Borrowings	525,000	
			Owners' Equity			Capital Stock Issue	766,030	
			Capital Stock	$766,030		Cash Dividends to Stockholders	0	1,591,030
			Retained Earnings	198,000	964,030			
			Total Liabilities & Owners' Equity		$2,198,740	Net Increase in Cash During Year		$ 243,000

A New Layout to Learn the Interlocking Nature of the Three Basic Financial Statements

Please look at Exhibit D on page 20. These are the same financial statements shown earlier, although they have been rearranged into a new layout.

First, the lines of connection between the three statements are drawn in; these serve as "tether lines" in the following discussion.

To help show these lines more clearly the Balance Sheet is positioned in the middle and it is shown in the one column (or, "report form") format—assets are on the top, and liabilities and stockholders' equity are on the bottom. The Income Statement is placed on the left and the Cash Flow Statement on the right.

Notice that the format of the Cash Flow Statement is changed quite a bit from that first introduced in Chapter 1. Basically, the Cash Flow Statement now uses the bottom-line net income from the Income Statement as the starting point. This net income figure is then "adjusted" to arrive at the cash outflow (in this example) from the profit-making operations of the company for the year.

In Exhibit D Accounts Payable and Accrued Expenses are divided into two parts each, to show the two separate sources of each (which are explained in later chapters). A few tether lines are not drawn in (they will be made clear in later chapters), to avoid crossing over too many other lines.

So now we have all three financial statements tied together, and the important relationships among the three are made clear. Remember, these statements are for the first year of business in this example.

Financial statements are *not* reported to managers or to creditors and investors in the manner shown in Exhibit D. Accountants assume that interested readers mentally fill in the lines of connection, and make the comparisons shown in Exhibit D. Accountants probably assume too much. It takes a fair amount of understanding and some experience to know which relationships are important to look for and what these comparisons mean.

Until managers and other users develop such skills in reading financial statements, the "octopus" format shown in Exhibit D, which shows the "tentacles" of connection, is very useful. The format certainly is helpful in explaining financial statements.

The Exhibit is repeated at the beginning of the following chapters, each of which focuses on one basic line of connection. For example, Chapter 4 explores the very important linkage between Sales Revenue in the Income Statement and Accounts Receivable in the Balance Sheet.

Exhibit D looks rather formidable at first glance, doesn't it? Like most reports with a lot of detail, you have to take it one piece at a time, rather than in one quick sweep. It's like looking at a chess board in the middle of a game. You have to study each piece in relation to the other relevant pieces before you can see the overall pattern and situation.

We'll go carefully through each step, one at a time, in the following chapters. This will take us through Chapter 16. Then we'll quickly repeat the main points for the second year of business.

EXHIBIT D—CHAPTER 4

INCOME STATEMENT FOR FIRST YEAR		
Sales Revenue		$4,212,000
Cost of Goods Sold Expense		2,740,400
Gross Margin		$1,471,600
Operating Expenses	$1,010,880	
Depreciation Expense	78,220	1,089,100
Operating Earnings		$ 382,500
Interest Expense		82,500
Earnings Before Income Tax		$ 300,000
Income Tax Expense		102,000
Net Income		$ 198,000

BALANCE SHEET AT END OF FIRST YEAR		
Cash		$ 243,000
Accounts Receivable		405,000
Inventory		632,400
Prepaid Expenses		77,760
Property, Plant & Equipment	$918,800	
Accumulated Depreciation	(78,220)	840,580
Total Assets		$2,198,740
Accounts Payable		
Inventory	$210,800	
Operating Expenses	58,320	$ 269,120
Accrued Expenses		
Operations	$116,640	
Interest	13,750	130,390
Income Tax Payable		10,200
Short-Term Notes Payable		300,000
Long-Term Notes Payable		525,000
Owners' Equity		
Capital Stock	$766,030	
Retained Earnings	198,000	964,030
Total Liabilities & Owners' Equity		$2,198,740

CASH FLOW STATEMENT FOR FIRST YEAR		
Cash Flows from Operating Activities		
Net Income	$198,000	
Accounts Receivable Increase	(405,000)	
Inventory Increase	(632,400)	
Prepaid Expenses Increase	(77,760)	
Depreciation Expense	78,220	
Accounts Payable Increase	269,120	
Accrued Expenses Increase	130,390	
Income Tax Payable Increase	10,200	($ 429,230)
Cash Flows from Investing Activities		
Purchases of Property, Plant & Equipment		(918,800)
Cash Flows from Financing Activities		
Short-Term Borrowings	$300,000	
Long-Term Borrowings	525,000	
Capital Stock Issue	766,030	
Cash Dividends to Stockholders	0	1,591,030
Net Increase in Cash During Year		$ 243,000

4

SALES REVENUE
↓
ACCOUNTS RECEIVABLE

Refer to Exhibit D—Chapter 4. This Exhibit, introduced in the preceding chapter, is presented here again for convenient reference. Because the Exhibit will be repeated in the following chapters also, the chapter number for which the Exhibit is being used is given.

Notice the two accounts connected in the Exhibit—Sales Revenue in the Income Statement and Accounts Receivable in the Balance Sheet. The relationship between the two and the nature of each are the main topics of this chapter. You'll notice that only this one line of connection is shown in the Exhibit, whereas all lines of connection are shown in the "master" Exhibit D on page 20.

In this example the company made total sales of $4,212,000 during the year. When a sale is made, the amount of the sale, which basically is sales price times the quantity sold, is recorded in Sales Revenue. This account accumulates all sales made during the year. At year-end, therefore, the balance in the account is the sum of all sales for the entire year.

Assume in this example that the company makes all its sales on credit. This means that cash is not received until sometime after the date of sale. The amount owed to the company, however, is immediately recorded in Accounts Receivable when each sale is made. The balance in this asset account is the amount of uncollected sales revenue.

Extending credit to customers creates a cash inflow lag. The balance of Accounts Receivable is the amount of this lag. Later, when cash is collected from customers, the Cash account is increased and Accounts Receivable is decreased.

By the end of the year most of the sales made during the year had been collected; the receivables had been converted into cash. But at year-end many sales had not yet been collected.

The amount of these uncollected sales is the balance of Accounts Receivable at the end of the year.

Some of its customers pay quickly, to take advantage of prompt payment discounts offered by the company. (These discounts reduce its sales prices, but speed up its cash receipts.) On the other hand, the typical customer waits about 5 weeks to pay the company, and foregoes the prompt payment discount. The really slow customers wait 10 weeks or more to pay the company.

In sum, the company has a mixture of quick, regular, and slow paying customers; we'll assume that the average sales credit period of this company is 5 weeks. Thus, 5 weeks of the company's sales for the year are still uncollected at year-end. So the ending balance of its Accounts Receivables is computed as follows in this example:

$$\frac{5}{52} \times \underset{\text{Sales Revenue for year}}{\$4,212,000} = \underset{\text{Accounts Receivable}}{\$405,000}$$

You'll notice in Exhibit D that the ending balance of Accounts Receivable is indeed $405,000.

The main point here is that the average sales credit period determines the size of Accounts Receivable relative to annual sales revenue. The longer the average sales credit period, the larger the Accounts Receivable.

Let's approach this key point from another direction. Using information in the financial statements, we can determine the average sales credit period. The first step is to compute the following ratio:

$$\frac{\$4,212,000 \text{ Sales Revenue for year}}{\$405,000 \text{ Accounts Receivable}} = 10.4$$

This computation gives the *Accounts Receivable turnover ratio*. This number divided into 52 weeks gives the average sales credit period expressed in number of weeks:

$$\frac{52 \text{ weeks}}{10.4 \text{ Accounts Receivable turnover ratio}} = 5 \text{ weeks}$$

Time is the essence of the matter here. What interests the manager, and the company's creditors and investors as well, is how long it takes on average to turn its receivables into cash. The Accounts Receivable turnover ratio is most meaningful when it is used to determine the number of weeks (or days) it takes the company to convert its receivables into cash.

You may argue that 5 weeks is too long an average sales credit period for the company. This is precisely the point: What should it be? The manager in charge has to decide whether the average sales credit period is getting out of hand. The manager can shorten credit terms, shut off credit to slow players, or step up collection efforts.

This is not the place to discuss customer credit policies relative to selling strategies and customer relations, which would take us far into the fields of marketing and credits and collections. But to make an important point here: Assume that without losing any sales the company's average sales credit period had been only 4 weeks, instead of the 5 weeks assumed in the financial statements of the company. In this case the ending balance of Accounts Receivable would have been $81,000 less, which is the average sales revenue per week ($4,212,000 ÷ 52 weeks = $81,000). The company would have collected $81,000 more cash during the year.

With such additional cash inflow the company could have borrowed $81,000 less. At a 10% annual interest rate this would have saved $8,100 interest expense before income tax. Or the owners could have invested $81,000 less in the business and put their money elsewhere. The point is, of course, that capital has a high cost. Excess Accounts Receivable means that excess debt, or excess owners' equity capital, is being used by the business.

A slow-up in collecting customers' receivables, or a deliberate shift in company policy allowing longer credit terms, would cause Accounts Receivable to increase. Additional capital would have to be secured, or the company would have to try to get by on a smaller cash balance.

If you were the manager in this example you would have to decide whether the size of Accounts Receivable, being 5 weeks of annual sales revenue, is consistent with the company's sales credit terms and collection policies. Perhaps 5 weeks is too long and you need to take action. If you were a creditor or an investor, you should be very interested in whether the manager is allowing the average sales credit period to get out of control. And you should be interested in any major change in the average sales credit period that may signal a major change in the company's policies.

EXHIBIT D—CHAPTER 5

INCOME STATEMENT FOR FIRST YEAR

Sales Revenue		$4,212,000
Cost of Goods Sold Expense		2,740,400
Gross Margin		$1,471,600
Operating Expenses	$1,010,880	
Depreciation Expense	78,220	1,089,100
Operating Earnings		$ 382,500
Interest Expense		82,500
Earnings Before Income Tax		$ 300,000
Income Tax Expense		102,000
Net Income		$ 198,000

BALANCE SHEET AT END OF FIRST YEAR

Cash		$ 243,000
Accounts Receivable		405,000
Inventory		632,400
Prepaid Expenses		77,760
Property, Plant & Equipment	$918,800	
Accumulated Depreciation	(78,220)	840,580
Total Assets		$2,198,740
Accounts Payable		
Inventory	$210,800	
Operating Expenses	58,320	$ 269,120
Accrued Expenses		
Operations	$116,640	
Interest	13,750	130,390
Income Tax Payable		10,200
Short-Term Notes Payable		300,000
Long-Term Notes Payable		525,000
Owners' Equity		
Capital Stock	$766,030	
Retained Earnings	198,000	964,030
Total Liabilities & Owners' Equity		$2,198,740

CASH FLOW STATEMENT FOR FIRST YEAR

Cash Flows from Operating Activities		
Net Income	$198,000	
Accounts Receivable Increase	(405,000)	
Inventory Increase	(632,400)	
Prepaid Expenses Increase	(77,760)	
Depreciation Expense	78,220	
Accounts Payable Increase	269,120	
Accrued Expenses Increase	130,390	
Income Tax Payable Increase	10,200	($ 429,230)
Cash Flows from Investing Activities		
Purchases of Property, Plant & Equipment		(918,800)
Cash Flows from Financing Activities		
Short-Term Borrowings	$300,000	
Long-Term Borrowings	525,000	
Capital Stock Issue	766,030	
Cash Dividends to Stockholders	0	1,591,030
Net Increase in Cash During Year		$ 243,000

COST OF GOODS SOLD EXPENSE

INVENTORY

To begin, refer to Exhibit D—Chapter 5. Notice the two accounts connected—Cost of Goods Sold Expense in the Income Statement and Inventory in the Balance Sheet. The relationship between these two accounts and the nature of each are the topics of this chapter.

Cost of Goods Sold Expense is, by far, the largest expense in the Income Statement. It's deducted from Sales Revenue to determine *gross margin*, which is the first of the four profit lines reported in the Income Statement.

Gross margin is called gross because no other expenses have been deducted. Only the cost of buying (or making) the product is deducted from sales revenue at this point. Gross margin is the starting point for earning an adequate final profit (net income). In other words, the first step is to sell the products (goods) for enough gross margin so that all the other expenses of the business can be covered. These other expenses are discussed in later chapters.

In this example the company earned a gross margin equal to 35% of its sales revenue:

$$\frac{\$1,471,600 \text{ Gross Margin}}{\$4,212,000 \text{ Sales Revenue}} = 35\% \text{ (rounded)}$$

The company sells a mix of different products, not all at the same gross profit margin (percent of sales price). In total, for all products sold during the year, its average gross profit is 35%, which is fairly typical for a broad cross section of businesses.

To sell products a business must carry a stock of products, on hand and ready for delivery to its customers. This stock of products, the goods being held for sale, is called *Inventory*. So making sales causes Inventory to appear in the Balance Sheet. The line of connection is not with Sales Revenue, but rather

with Cost of Goods Sold Expense, because Inventory is reported at cost in the Balance Sheet, *not* at its sales value.

When a company buys products, its Inventory account is increased by the cost of the goods. This cost is kept in the Inventory asset account until the items are sold and delivered to customers when making sales. At this time the cost is removed from the asset and charged to Cost of Goods Sold Expense. (If products become definitely unsalable or are stolen, their cost is removed from Inventory and charged to expense.)

The Inventory balance at year-end—$632,400 in this example, as shown in Exhibit D—is the cost of products awaiting sale next year. The $2,740,400 deducted from Sales Revenue in the Income Statement is the cost of the goods that were sold during the year; of course, none of these products are on hand in Inventory at year-end.

Some of the company's products may come in and go out in a week or two; other goods may stay in stock 4 months or longer. As usual, holding periods differ for different products. The company's average inventory holding period, given the mix of all its products, is assumed to be 12 weeks in this example.

In other words, the quantity of goods in inventory is enough for 12 weeks of average sales. As just mentioned, inventory is recorded at cost. So 12 weeks of sales here means 12 weeks of cost of goods sold, not 12 weeks of sales revenue. Knowing that the average inventory holding period is 12 weeks, the company's Inventory balance is computed as follows in this example:

$$\frac{12}{52} \times \$2,740,400 \qquad\qquad = \$632,400$$
$$\text{Cost of Goods Sold for year} \qquad \text{Inventory}$$

You'll notice in Exhibit D that the ending balance of Inventory is indeed $632,400.

The main point is that the average inventory holding period determines the size of Inventory relative to annual cost of goods sold. The longer the holding period, the larger the Inventory.

Let's approach this key point from another direction. Using information available from the financial statements, we can determine the average inventory holding period. The first step is to compute the following ratio:

$$\frac{\$2,740,400 \text{ Cost of Goods Sold Expense for year}}{\$632,400 \text{ Inventory}} = 4.33$$

This gives the *Inventory turnover ratio*. This number divided into 52 weeks gives the average inventory holding period expressed in number of weeks:

$$\frac{52 \text{ weeks}}{4.33 \text{ Inventory turnover ratio}} = 12 \text{ weeks}$$

Time is the essence of the matter here, as it is with the average sales credit period discussed in the preceding chapter. What interests the manager, and the company's creditors and investors as well, is how long the company holds an average item of inventory before it's sold. The Inventory turnover ratio is most meaningful when it is used to determine the number of weeks (or days) it takes the company before the inventory is sold.

Is 12 weeks too long? Should the company's average inventory holding period be shorter? This is precisely the key question that business managers, creditors, and investors should be concerned with. If the holding period is longer than really necessary, too much capital is being tied up in inventory, and, as already mentioned, capital has a high cost. Or the company may be cash poor because it has too much money in inventory and not enough in the bank.

If the company could reduce its inventory holding period to, say, 10 weeks, $105,400 capital would be saved ($52,700 Cost of Goods Sold Expense per week × 2 weeks less Inventory = $105,400 less capital required). However, with only 10 weeks average inventory, the company may be unable to make many sales because certain products were not available when needed. In other words, if the average inventory holding period is too low, the result may be *stock-outs* of certain goods, or not being able to get the goods as soon as needed to make sales. The cost of carrying inventory has to be balanced against the profit opportunities lost by not having the products in stock ready for sale.

In short, managers, and creditors and investors as well, should be concerned that the average inventory holding period is neither too high nor too low. If too high, capital is being wasted; if too low, profit opportunities are being missed. Comparisons with other companies in the same line of business and historical trends provide the guidelines for testing a company's inventory holding period.

EXHIBIT D—CHAPTER 6

INCOME STATEMENT FOR FIRST YEAR		
Sales Revenue		$4,212,000
Cost of Goods Sold Expense		2,740,400
Gross Margin		$1,471,600
Operating Expenses	$1,010,880	
Depreciation Expense	78,220	1,089,100
Operating Earnings		$ 382,500
Interest Expense		82,500
Earnings Before Income Tax		$ 300,000
Income Tax Expense		102,000
Net Income		$ 198,000

BALANCE SHEET AT END OF FIRST YEAR		
Cash		$ 243,000
Accounts Receivable		405,000
Inventory		632,400
Prepaid Expenses		77,760
Property, Plant & Equipment	$918,800	
Accumulated Depreciation	(78,220)	840,580
Total Assets		$2,198,740
Accounts Payable		
Inventory	$210,800	
Operating Expenses	58,320	$ 269,120
Accrued Expenses		
Operations	$116,640	
Interest	13,750	130,390
Income Tax Payable		10,200
Short-Term Notes Payable		300,000
Long-Term Notes Payable		525,000
Owners' Equity		
Capital Stock	$766,030	
Retained Earnings	198,000	964,030
Total Liabilities & Owners' Equity		$2,198,740

CASH FLOW STATEMENT FOR FIRST YEAR		
Cash Flows from Operating Activities		
Net Income	$198,000	
Accounts Receivable Increase	(405,000)	
Inventory Increase	(632,400)	
Prepaid Expenses Increase	(77,760)	
Depreciation Expense	78,220	
Accounts Payable Increase	269,120	
Accrued Expenses Increase	130,390	
Income Tax Payable Increase	10,200	($ 429,230)
Cash Flows from Investing Activities		
Purchases of Property, Plant & Equipment		(918,800)
Cash Flows from Financing Activities		
Short-Term Borrowings	$300,000	
Long-Term Borrowings	525,000	
Capital Stock Issue	766,030	
Cash Dividends to Stockholders	0	1,591,030
Net Increase in Cash During Year		$ 243,000

6

INVENTORY

↓

ACCOUNTS PAYABLE

Please note in Exhibit D—Chapter 6 the line linking Inventory with Accounts Payable in the Balance Sheet.

To set the stage here, let's review very briefly the last two chapters. The sales prices of goods (products) sold are accumulated in the Sales Revenue account. Sales made on credit cause Accounts Receivable; the longer the credit period, the larger the Accounts Receivable. The cost of goods sold is accumulated in the Cost of Goods Sold Expense account. Products must be bought and held in Inventory before they are sold. The longer the holding period, the larger the Inventory.

Inventory is closely related to Cost of Goods Sold Expense; it's also closely related to Accounts Payable. This second relationship is the main topic of this chapter.

Businesses purchase their inventory on credit. COD (cash on delivery) purchase terms are not often encountered, unless a company is in financial trouble or has a lousy credit rating. So the typical business does not make immediate payment for its inventory purchases. (Manufacturers buy their raw materials and production supplies on credit; the main points in the following discussion apply to these types of items as well.)

When inventory is purchased on credit, the liability for the amount of goods bought is recorded in *Accounts Payable*. As mentioned in the preceding chapter, the cost is also recorded in Inventory; both the asset and the liability increase the same amount.

Some purchases are paid quickly, to take advantage of prompt payment discounts offered by suppliers. But many bills are not paid until 2 months or so after purchase. Based on its payments experience and policies, a business can determine the average credit period it waits before paying for its inventory purchases. In this example, we'll assume that the average inventory purchases credit period is 4 weeks.

In other words, from the date of purchase to the date of payment is 4 weeks on average. So the last 4 weeks of inventory purchases had not been paid yet at year-end. Purchases may vary week to week; in this example, however, we assume that after the initial inventory build-up early in the year, purchases since then have been fairly equal week to week to replace goods sold and keep inventory at a stable level.

The average cost of goods sold per week (equal to purchases per week here) is $52,700 ($2,740,400 cost of goods sold per year ÷ 52 weeks = $52,700). So the Accounts Payable amount from inventory purchases is computed as follows in this example:

$52,700	× 4 weeks	= $210,800
Cost of Goods	inventory	Accounts Payable
Sold (and	purchase	
purchases per	credit	
week)	period	

See this connection in Exhibit D.

Sometimes at year-end the amount of Accounts Payable from inventory purchases may be higher than normal. The company may have made a large purchase just before year-end because of a supply shortage forecast or in anticipation of price increases. Or, the company may have deliberately slowed down payment of its bills toward year-end to conserve its cash balance, which would cause a temporary bulge in Accounts Payable.

EXHIBIT D—CHAPTER 7

INCOME STATEMENT FOR FIRST YEAR

Sales Revenue		$4,212,000
Cost of Goods Sold Expense		2,740,400
Gross Margin		$1,471,600
Operating Expenses	$1,010,880	
Depreciation Expense	78,220	1,089,100
Operating Earnings		$ 382,500
Interest Expense		82,500
Earnings Before Income Tax		$ 300,000
Income Tax Expense		102,000
Net Income		$ 198,000

BALANCE SHEET AT END OF FIRST YEAR

Cash		$ 243,000
Accounts Receivable		405,000
Inventory		632,400
Prepaid Expenses		77,760
Property, Plant & Equipment	$918,800	
Accumulated Depreciation	(78,220)	840,580
Total Assets		$2,198,740
Accounts Payable		
Inventory	$210,800	
Operating Expenses	58,320	$ 269,120
Accrued Expenses		
Operations	$116,640	
Interest	13,750	130,390
Income Tax Payable		10,200
Short-Term Notes Payable		300,000
Long-Term Notes Payable		525,000
Owners' Equity		
Capital Stock	$766,030	
Retained Earnings	198,000	964,030
Total Liabilities & Owners' Equity		$2,198,740

CASH FLOW STATEMENT FOR FIRST YEAR

Cash Flows from Operating Activities		
Net Income	$198,000	
Accounts Receivable Increase	(405,000)	
Inventory Increase	(632,400)	
Prepaid Expenses Increase	(77,760)	
Depreciation Expense	78,220	
Accounts Payable Increase	269,120	
Accrued Expenses Increase	130,390	
Income Tax Payable Increase	10,200	($ 429,230)
Cash Flows from Investing Activities		
Purchases of Property, Plant & Equipment		(918,800)
Cash Flows from Financing Activities		
Short-Term Borrowings	$300,000	
Long-Term Borrowings	525,000	
Capital Stock Issue	766,030	
Cash Dividends to Stockholders	0	1,591,030
Net Increase in Cash During Year		$ 243,000

7

OPERATING EXPENSES

↓

ACCOUNTS PAYABLE

Have you looked at Exhibit D—Chapter 7? Note the linkage between Operating Expenses in the Income Statement and Accounts Payable in the Balance Sheet. This relationship and the nature of these two accounts are discussed in this chapter.

Operating Expenses is a conglomerate account in the Income Statement, which includes all the different expenses of running the business *except* Depreciation Expense. The Depreciation Expense is unique and is reported separately from the Operating Expenses. Depreciation is discussed in Chapter 10.

Included under the umbrella of Operating Expenses are the following (in no particular order):

◆ Rent of land and buildings

◆ Wages and salaries paid officers, office employees, salespersons, warehouse workers, and so on

◆ Payroll taxes and other fringe benefit costs of labor

◆ Office and data processing supplies and machine rentals

◆ Property taxes

◆ Telephone

◆ Utilities (water, gas, electricity)

◆ General liability insurance, and fire insurance on contents, buildings, and property owned by the business

◆ Advertising and sales promotion costs

◆ Bad debts (credit sales never collected)

Many other specific operating expenses could be listed.

One reason for grouping all operating expenses (except depreciation) into one total account in the Income Statement is that the basic accounting for all these expenses can be explained in the same way. This chapter explains how operating expenses affect *Accounts Payable*. The next two chapters explain how operating expenses also affect two other Balance Sheet accounts.

It would be simple if every dollar of operating expenses charged to the year also were a dollar actually paid out in that same year. It would be nice and easy to equate operating expenses with cash disbursements; no other Balance Sheet (except Cash) would be affected by these expenses. But it's not quite that simple. Many operating expenses must be recorded *before* they are paid.

For example, on December 27 the company receives a bill from the utility company for power usage during the month period ending December 20. (Assume the company's accounting year ends December 31.) The amount of this expense clearly belongs in this year, so it is recorded in Accounts Payable.

This is just one example of many such unpaid operating expenses at the end of a company's accounting year. Other examples are bills from lawyers and CPAs for services, bills from newspapers for advertisements already run in the papers, telephone bills, and so on. Generally speaking, the credit terms of these payables are not long, 1 to 4 weeks being typical.

In this example we'll assume that the average credit period of the company's payables from unpaid operating expenses is 3 weeks. So, 3 weeks of its total operating expenses for the year are in Accounts Payable at year-end. In this example the average amount of operating expenses per week is $19,440 ($1,010,880 operating expenses for year ÷ 52 weeks = $19,440).

The amount of Accounts Payable at year-end from operating expenses is computed as follows:

$19,440   × 3 weeks average = $58,320
Operating Expenses   credit period   Accounts Payable
per week

See in Exhibit D that this amount is included in Accounts Payable.

Recall that inventory purchases on credit are also recorded in Accounts Payable. This liability account thus has a total balance of $269,120 at year-end ($210,800 from inventory purchases + $58,320 from operating expenses).

Every bill (or invoice) for goods or services received by the business is recorded in Accounts Payable. The immediate recording of these bills is necessary to recognize the liability and to recognize the increase of inventory or the increase of operating expense. However, the recording of these payables does *not* decrease Cash; there is no cash outflow. This very important point is discussed in Chapter 14, which deals with the cash flow analysis of net income.

EXHIBIT D—CHAPTER 8

INCOME STATEMENT FOR FIRST YEAR		
Sales Revenue		$4,212,000
Cost of Goods Sold Expense		2,740,400
Gross Margin		$1,471,600
Operating Expenses	$1,010,880	
Depreciation Expense	78,220	1,089,100
Operating Earnings		$ 382,500
Interest Expense		82,500
Earnings Before Income Tax		$ 300,000
Income Tax Expense		102,000
Net Income		$ 198,000

BALANCE SHEET AT END OF FIRST YEAR		
Cash		$ 243,000
Accounts Receivable		405,000
Inventory		632,400
Prepaid Expenses		77,760
Property, Plant & Equipment	$918,800	
Accumulated Depreciation	(78,220)	840,580
Total Assets		$2,198,740
Accounts Payable		
Inventory	$210,800	
Operating Expenses	58,320	$ 269,120
Accrued Expenses		
Operations	$116,640	
Interest	13,750	130,390
Income Tax Payable		10,200
Short-Term Notes Payable		300,000
Long-Term Notes Payable		525,000
Owners' Equity		
Capital Stock	$766,030	
Retained Earnings	198,000	964,030
Total Liabilities & Owners' Equity		$2,198,740

CASH FLOW STATEMENT FOR FIRST YEAR		
Cash Flows from Operating Activities		
Net Income	$198,000	
Accounts Receivable Increase	(405,000)	
Inventory Increase	(632,400)	
Prepaid Expenses Increase	(77,760)	
Depreciation Expense	78,220	
Accounts Payable Increase	269,120	
Accrued Expenses Increase	130,390	
Income Tax Payable Increase	10,200	($ 429,230)
Cash Flows from Investing Activities		
Purchases of Property, Plant & Equipment		(918,800)
Cash Flows from Financing Activities		
Short-Term Borrowings	$300,000	
Long-Term Borrowings	525,000	
Capital Stock Issue	766,030	
Cash Dividends to Stockholders	0	1,591,030
Net Increase in Cash During Year		$ 243,000

8

OPERATING EXPENSES

$\downarrow$

ACCRUED EXPENSES (PAYABLE)

Refer to the connection in Exhibit D—Chapter 8 linking Operating Expenses in the Income Statement with Accrued Expenses in the Balance Sheet.

Now let's return to the utility expense example discussed in Chapter 7. Clearly, the utility cost through December 20 should be recorded in expense for the year. The utilities have been used in the operations of the business, and an actual bill has been received that is a clear and definite liability of the business. Now what about the utility usage from December 20 through December 31? The cost of utility usage for this last third of the month has not yet been billed to the business, nor even measured by the utility company, for that matter.

The accountant estimates the amount of this expense for the last third of December and records this amount so that total operating expenses include the full amount for the entire year. However, by December 31 no bill had been received from the utility company. The company had a liability for sure—an *unbilled* liability. So a different type of liability is recorded, called *Accrued Expenses*.

The Accrued Expenses liability is separated from Accounts Payable for two reasons. First, the amounts recorded in the Accrued Expenses liability are *estimates*, which depend on the methods and reliability of the methods used to make the estimates. In contrast, the amounts recorded in Accounts Payable are definite amounts. Second, the Accounts Payable are actual bills (invoices) in the hands of the company; Accrued Expenses are liabilities for which no bills have been received.

What are some of the estimated liabilities recorded in Accrued Expenses? More than you probably would guess. In addition to the utility expense example discussed above, the Accrued Expenses liability usually includes the following:

- Accumulated vacation and sick leave pay earned by employees, which has not yet been paid by the company; this can add up to a sizable amount

- Unpaid sales commissions earned by the company's salespersons that will be paid later

- Portions of annual property taxes that should be charged to this year that haven't been billed to the company yet

- Partial-month telephone costs that have been incurred but not yet billed to the company at year-end

In summary, about a third-month of utility cost, perhaps a half-month of telephone cost, maybe a half-year of employees' vacation cost, and several other such accumulated expenses are recorded in the Accrued Expenses at the end of the year. Not recording these liabilities would have caused a serious error in the profit measure for the year. Moreover, these are real liabilities, even though the amounts are estimated and no bills have been received.

In this example the average time before paying these liabilities is assumed to be 6 weeks. In other words, 6 weeks of its annual operating expenses are in Accrued Expenses at year-end. As computed in Chapter 7, the average operating expenses per week is $19,440 (see page 36). So the amount of Accrued Expenses from operating expenses is computed as follows:

$19,440	× 6 weeks	= $116,640
Operating Expenses per week	average credit period	Accrued Expenses

See in Exhibit D that the Accrued Expenses balance includes this amount.

The Accrued Expenses amount relative to total annual operating expenses may be more or less than 6 weeks for another business. Experience provides the guideline for each individual business. For many businesses 6 weeks is about right, even though this ratio may look rather high, especially if we consider both the Accrued Expenses (estimated unbilled liabilities) and Accounts Payable (definite billed liabilities). In Chapter 7 we see that 3 weeks of our company's total annual operating expenses are in Accounts Payable at year-end, and in this chapter we see that 6 weeks are in Accrued Expenses at year-end.

In summary, 9 weeks of the company's total operating expenses for the year are unpaid at year-end, which relieved the company of having to come up with this much cash for operating expenses during the year. The company avoided $174,960 of cash payout during the year ($58,320 Accounts Payable plus $116,640 Accrued Expenses).

If the company could have stretched the average wait (or credit period) for paying its operating expenses from 9 weeks to, say, 11 weeks, it could have avoided an additional $38,880 of cash disbursements ($19,440 average operating expenses per week $\times$ 2 additional weeks of waiting to pay the expenses = $38,880). So the Accounts Payable and Accrued Expenses resulting from operating expenses have a significant impact on cash flow. Any change in the size of these two liabilities relative to annual operating expenses has a cash flow impact that should not be ignored by the company's managers, as well as the creditors and investors who use its financial statements.

In Exhibit D you probably have noticed that there is another, though much smaller, source of Accrued Expenses—that is, the unpaid interest expense at year-end. This is discussed in Chapter 11.

Accrued Expenses and Accounts Payable result from the normal delay in paying for operating expenses. The expense is recorded now but paid for later; the liability bridges the two dates. In contrast, some expenses are paid for now but not recorded as an expense (deduction against sales revenue) until later. This reverse situation is discussed in the next chapter.

EXHIBIT D—CHAPTER 9

INCOME STATEMENT FOR FIRST YEAR

Sales Revenue		$4,212,000
Cost of Goods Sold Expense		2,740,400
Gross Margin		$1,471,600
Operating Expenses	$1,010,880	
Depreciation Expense	78,220	1,089,100
Operating Earnings		$ 382,500
Interest Expense		82,500
Earnings Before Income Tax		$ 300,000
Income Tax Expense		102,000
Net Income		$ 198,000

BALANCE SHEET AT END OF FIRST YEAR

Cash		$ 243,000
Accounts Receivable		405,000
Inventory		632,400
Prepaid Expenses		77,760
Property, Plant & Equipment	$918,800	
Accumulated Depreciation	(78,220)	840,580
Total Assets		$2,198,740
Accounts Payable		
Inventory	$210,800	
Operating Expenses	58,320	$ 269,120
Accrued Expenses		
Operations	$116,640	
Interest	13,750	130,390
Income Tax Payable		10,200
Short-Term Notes Payable		300,000
Long-Term Notes Payable		525,000
Owners' Equity		
Capital Stock	$766,030	
Retained Earnings	198,000	964,030
Total Liabilities & Owners' Equity		$2,198,740

CASH FLOW STATEMENT FOR FIRST YEAR

Cash Flows from Operating Activities		
Net Income	$198,000	
Accounts Receivable Increase	(405,000)	
Inventory Increase	(632,400)	
Prepaid Expenses Increase	(77,760)	
Depreciation Expense	78,220	
Accounts Payable Increase	269,120	
Accrued Expenses Increase	130,390	
Income Tax Payable Increase	10,200	($ 429,230)
Cash Flows from Investing Activities		
Purchases of Property, Plant & Equipment		(918,800)
Cash Flows from Financing Activities		
Short-Term Borrowings	$300,000	
Long-Term Borrowings	525,000	
Capital Stock Issue	766,030	
Cash Dividends to Stockholders	0	1,591,030
Net Increase in Cash During Year		$ 243,000

9

OPERATING EXPENSES

↕

PREPAID EXPENSES

To begin, refer to the connection in Exhibit D—Chapter 9 linking Operating Expenses in the Income Statement with Prepaid Expenses in the Balance Sheet. The title of the chapter means that certain operating expenses cause Prepaid Expenses to appear in the Balance Sheet. However, the actual sequence of events is that certain operating costs are first paid in advance (prepaid), and then not until later are they charged off to expense.

Several operating costs must be paid for *before* these costs should be recorded as expense. There is a cash outlay before the amount should be recorded as an expense (as a deduction against sales revenue to measure profit for the period). For example, insurance premiums must be paid in advance of the insurance policy period. Office supplies are bought in quantities that last 2 to 3 months. Annual property taxes frequently are paid at the start of the tax assessment year. There are many more such examples of what are called *Prepaid Expenses*.

When paid, the cost is initially recorded in Prepaid Expenses, which is an asset account. The amount is allocated so that each future month receives its "fair share" of the cost. Each month the appropriate part of the cost is taken out of Prepaid Expenses and recorded in expense. All of the costs initially recorded in Prepaid Expenses are later taken out and put in expense in the correct months.

Based on its experience and operations, a company can determine how large, on average, its Prepaid Expenses balance is relative to its annual operating expenses. We'll assume that the company's Prepaid Expenses in this example equals 4 weeks of its annual operating expenses. Previously (page 36) we computed that the operating expenses per week are $19,440. So the Prepaid Expenses balance is computed as follows:

$$\underset{\substack{\text{Operating Expenses} \\ \text{per week}}}{\$19,440} \times 4 \text{ weeks} = \underset{\text{Prepaid Expenses}}{\$77,760}$$

See in Exhibit D that $77,760 is the balance of the Prepaid Expenses account.

In summary, the company in the example had to prepay one month of its annual operating expenses. This is a demand on cash during the year, in the amount of $77,760. If the manager could have reduced these prepayments to, say, only 3 weeks of the annual operating expenses (instead of 4 weeks in the example), the Prepaid Expenses would have been only $58,320 ($19,440 operating expenses per week × 3 weeks = $58,320). This would have reduced the demand on cash by $19,440, or one week of operating expenses.

On the other hand, if prepayments had been 3 weeks higher, say 7 weeks instead of 4 weeks in the example, the cash demand would have been $58,320 more. The cash flow impact of Prepaid Expenses is explained further in Chapter 14.

EXHIBIT D—CHAPTER 10

INCOME STATEMENT FOR FIRST YEAR

Sales Revenue		$4,212,000
Cost of Goods Sold Expense		2,740,400
Gross Margin		$1,471,600
Operating Expenses	$1,010,880	
Depreciation Expense	78,220	1,089,100
Operating Earnings		$ 382,500
Interest Expense		82,500
Earnings Before Income Tax		$ 300,000
Income Tax Expense		102,000
Net Income		$ 198,000

BALANCE SHEET AT END OF FIRST YEAR

Cash		$ 243,000
Accounts Receivable		405,000
Inventory		632,400
Prepaid Expenses		77,760
Property, Plant & Equipment	$918,800	
Accumulated Depreciation	(78,220)	840,580
Total Assets		$2,198,740
Accounts Payable		
Inventory	$210,800	
Operating Expenses	58,320	$ 269,120
Accrued Expenses		
Operations	$116,640	
Interest	13,750	130,390
Income Tax Payable		10,200
Short-Term Notes Payable		300,000
Long-Term Notes Payable		525,000
Owners' Equity		
Capital Stock	$766,030	
Retained Earnings	198,000	964,030
Total Liabilities & Owners' Equity		$2,198,740

CASH FLOW STATEMENT FOR FIRST YEAR

Cash Flows from Operating Activities		
Net Income	$198,000	
Accounts Receivable Increase	(405,000)	
Inventory Increase	(632,400)	
Prepaid Expenses Increase	(77,760)	
Depreciation Expense	78,220	
Accounts Payable Increase	269,120	
Accrued Expenses Increase	130,390	
Income Tax Payable Increase	10,200	($ 429,230)
Cash Flows from Investing Activities		
Purchases of Property, Plant & Equipment		(918,800)
Cash Flows from Financing Activities		
Short-Term Borrowings	$300,000	
Long-Term Borrowings	525,000	
Capital Stock Issue	766,030	
Cash Dividends to Stockholders	0	1,591,030
Net Increase in Cash During Year		$ 243,000

10

PROPERTY, PLANT & EQUIPMENT

$\downarrow$

DEPRECIATION

$\downarrow$

ACCUMULATED DEPRECIATION

A Brief Review of Expense Accounting

By now you should have sensed the basic logic of expense accounting. Expenses are not necessarily recorded when they happen to be paid; expenses are not recorded on a cash basis. Expenses are recorded either on a *matching of costs with sales revenues* basis or on a *cost of period* basis. Each basis is explained briefly here:

1. *Matching of costs with sales revenue basis*—cost of goods sold expense, sales commissions expense, and all other expenses directly identifiable with making sales are recorded in the same period as the sales revenue. The purpose is to match these costs with related sales revenue to get the correct measure of profit from sales.

2. *Cost of period basis*—many expenses are not directly identifiable with particular sales, such as office employees' salaries, rent of building space, data processing and record-keeping, legal and audit, insurance, interest on borrowed money, and many more. Nondirect expenses are just as necessary as direct expenses. But there is no way to match them with individual sales. So the nondirect expenses are recorded in the period in which benefit or use to the operations of the business takes place. For example, $1/12$ of the annual fire insurance premium is allocated to each month, office supplies are expensed in the month used, and so on.

The timing of expense recordings to match the expense with the correct sales revenue or to put the expense in the correct time period involves the use of asset and liability accounts. We have already discussed the use of Inventory and Prepaid Expenses for this purpose, as well as the Accounts Payable and Accrued Expenses liabilities. One type of asset not yet discussed is *Property, Plant & Equipment*, which we now turn to.

Depreciation Expense

In this example the company owns its real estate (land and buildings), as well as the other long-lived assets needed in its operations. For example, this company owns desks, cash registers, a computer system, trucks, display cabinets, shelving, various machines and tools, and so on.

These several different assets are grouped together under the heading Property, Plant & Equipment, which has a balance of $918,800 at the end of the first year. Please see Exhibit D—Chapter 10.

You may also want to refer to Exhibit B on page 10 again, which shows the classified Balance Sheet of the company. Notice that in the Balance Sheet these assets are reported in a more descriptive account called *Land, Building, Machines, Equipment, and Furniture*, which is positioned under the Property, Plant & Equipment heading.

Long-lived assets are used several years, but eventually they wear out or otherwise lose their usefulness to the business. In short, these assets have a limited life span of business (economic) usefulness. For instance, a typewriter will be disposed of sometime; it won't last forever.

The cost of the typewriter is prorated over each future year of expected use to the business. How many years? This is hardly more than an educated guess. As a practical matter the minimum, or shortest lives allowed for federal income tax purposes usually are the useful life estimates adopted by a business to depreciate their long-term operating assets in their financial statements.

The Tax Reform Act (TRA) of 1986 made major changes in allowable life estimates. Buildings have a useful life of 31.5 years. Cars and light trucks have 5-year useful lives. Most equipment and machinery falls in either the 7- or 10-years useful life category.

The logic of the tax law is based on the Accelerated Cost Recovery System (ACRS), which means that the business should recover the cost invested in its long-term operating assets by depreciating the cost of the assets over their useful lives.

"Accelerated" means that the tax law permits the assets to be depreciated faster than they actually wear out. For example, most buildings are still valuable after 31.5 years of use—though some might be torn down before then.

Accelerated also means that assets (except buildings) can be depreciated according to a front-end loading method whereby more depreciation is recorded in the earlier years than the later years of the assets' useful lives.

In this example the total depreciation expense recorded in the first year of business is $78,220, which is based on the ACRS lives permitted by the tax law. See Exhibit D again; notice depreciation expense in the Income Statement of this amount. One major asset (its building) is depreciated by the straight-line method, whereas its other assets (trucks and equipment, for example) are depreciated according to an accelerated, or front-end loading method. Depreciation expense methods are discussed further in Chapter 22.

The amount of depreciation expense charged to each year is relatively arbitrary compared to other expenses. One reason is that the useful life estimates are arbitrary. For a 12-months' insurance policy, there's little doubt that the total premium cost should be allocated over exactly 12 months. But long-lived assets, such as an office desk, display shelving, file cabinets, computers, or typewriters, present much more difficult problems. How long will these assets be used?

Given the inherent problems of estimating useful lives, financial statement readers are well advised to keep in mind the consequences of wrong estimates. If the useful life estimates are too short, depreciation expense each year is too high. In fact, useful life estimates are generally too short. Accountants, with the blessing of the Internal Revenue Code, favor this more conservative approach.

The Accumulated Depreciation Account

The amount of depreciation expense each year is not recorded as a decrease in the asset account directly. Instead, each year the amount of depreciation expense is added to the Accumulated Depreciation account. The balance in this account is deducted from the original cost of the assets (see Exhibit D). The remainder—$840,580 in this example—is called the *book value*. It's the undepreciated part of the assets' original cost, or future depreciation expense if you would.

The Accumulated Depreciation balance is the total depreciation recorded in this and previous years. In Exhibit D only 1 year of depreciation expense has been recorded because the business has been in operation only one year. So the Accumulated Depreciation account shows only the first year's depreciation amount. At the end of the second year, this account will show the total of the first and second years' depreciation expense.

Book Values of Long-Lived Assets
Compared with Their Replacement Costs

After several years the original cost of the long-lived assets reported in a company's Balance Sheet may be quite low compared to the current replacement costs of equivalent new long-lived assets. Inflation has hit these asset costs as much or more than everything else. The original cost amounts reported in a Balance Sheet are not meant to be indicators of the current replacement costs of the assets.

When looking ahead, managers, creditors, and investors should realize that the future replacement costs of these assets will be much higher than the historical costs reported in the Balance Sheet. For management purposes every year or two

it's a good idea to make an estimate of the current replacement costs of the business's long-lived operating assets. This does not and should not lead to a write-up of the assets in the Balance Sheet. This would be against generally accepted accounting principles.

Many business managers and many accountants have argued that such assets should be written up once every year to keep up with inflation, and that the depreciation expense each year should be based on the higher values. So far Congress has rejected this method for federal income tax purposes.

Nevertheless, the matter has been one of very serious and

continuing concern to the accounting profession, even though many doubt the usefulness of such information to investors. Somewhat as an experiment, the rule-making body of the accounting profession several years ago passed a requirement that large (indeed, very large!) public corporations must provide *supplementary* information about the current costs of their long-lived operating assets. However, this requirement was later repealed.

EXHIBIT D—CHAPTER 11

INCOME STATEMENT FOR FIRST YEAR		
Sales Revenue		$4,212,000
Cost of Goods Sold Expense		2,740,400
Gross Margin		$1,471,600
Operating Expenses	$1,010,880	
Depreciation Expense	78,220	1,089,100
Operating Earnings		$ 382,500
Interest Expense		82,500
Earnings Before Income Tax		$ 300,000
Income Tax Expense		102,000
Net Income		$ 198,000

BALANCE SHEET AT END OF FIRST YEAR		
Cash		$ 243,000
Accounts Receivable		405,000
Inventory		632,400
Prepaid Expenses		77,760
Property, Plant & Equipment	$918,800	
Accumulated Depreciation	(78,220)	840,580
Total Assets		$2,198,740
Accounts Payable		
Inventory	$210,800	
Operating Expenses	58,320	$ 269,120
Accrued Expenses		
Operations	$116,640	
Interest	13,750	130,390
Income Tax Payable		10,200
Short-Term Notes Payable		300,000
Long-Term Notes Payable		525,000
Owners' Equity		
Capital Stock	$766,030	
Retained Earnings	198,000	964,030
Total Liabilities & Owners' Equity		$2,198,740

CASH FLOW STATEMENT FOR FIRST YEAR		
Cash Flows from Operating Activities		
Net Income	$198,000	
Accounts Receivable Increase	(405,000)	
Inventory Increase	(632,400)	
Prepaid Expenses Increase	(77,760)	
Depreciation Expense	78,220	
Accounts Payable Increase	269,120	
Accrued Expenses Increase	130,390	
Income Tax Payable Increase	10,200	($ 429,230)
Cash Flows from Investing Activities		
Purchases of Property, Plant & Equipment		(918,800)
Cash Flows from Financing Activities		
Short-Term Borrowings	$300,000	
Long-Term Borrowings	525,000	
Capital Stock Issue	766,030	
Cash Dividends to Stockholders	0	1,591,030
Net Increase in Cash During Year		$ 243,000

11

INTEREST EXPENSE
↓
ACCRUED EXPENSES (PAYABLE)

It's a rare business that doesn't borrow money, in addition to having Accounts Payable and Accrued Expenses liabilities. A *note* (or similar legal instrument) is signed when borrowing; hence the liabilities from borrowing are called *Notes Payable*. One main difference is that interest is paid on borrowed money of course, whereas no interest is paid on Accounts Payable and Accrued Expenses. Notes Payable are always reported separately from non-interest-bearing liabilities in the Balance Sheet.

Interest is a charge per day for the use of borrowed money. Every day the money is borrowed means that more interest is owed. The ratio of interest to the amount borrowed is called the interest rate, and always is stated as a percent. Percent means "per hundred." If you borrow $100,000 for one year and pay $12,000 interest, the rate (ratio) of interest is: $12,000 interest ÷ $100,000 borrowed = $12 per $100, or 12%. Interest rates are stated as annual rates, even though the term of borrowing is shorter or longer than 1 year.

Interest is reported as a separate expense in the Income Statement. It's not the size of interest relative to other expenses, but its special nature that requires this separate disclosure. Interest is a financial cost as opposed to an operating cost; interest depends on the financial policies of the business regarding borrowing, not on its methods of operations.

When interest is paid *depends*. On short-term notes (less than 1 year periods) interest is paid in one sum at the maturity date of the note, which is the last day of the loan period. On longer-term notes, say for 5 or 10 years, interest is paid usually every 6 months, although monthly or quarterly interest payments are not unheard of. On both short-term and long-term notes there is a lag, or delay in paying interest. But the interest expense should be recorded for all days the money was borrowed.

The accumulated amount of unpaid interest expense at the end of the accounting period is recorded in *Accrued Expenses*, which is a liability account. In this example the company's interest expense is $6,875 per month. Due to the lag in paying interest, 2 months expense is unpaid at year-end, so:

$6,875 × 2 months = $13,750
Interest Expense   Accrued Expenses
per month

See the connection in Exhibit D.

You'll notice that Accrued Expenses now has a total balance of $130,390—the $13,750 unpaid interest expense plus the $116,640 unpaid operating expenses that were discussed earlier in Chapter 8.

EXHIBIT D—CHAPTER 12

INCOME STATEMENT FOR FIRST YEAR

Sales Revenue		$4,212,000
Cost of Goods Sold Expense		2,740,400
Gross Margin		$1,471,600
Operating Expenses	$1,010,880	
Depreciation Expense	78,220	1,089,100
Operating Earnings		$ 382,500
Interest Expense		82,500
Earnings Before Income Tax		$ 300,000
Income Tax Expense		102,000
Net Income		$ 198,000

BALANCE SHEET AT END OF FIRST YEAR

Cash		$ 243,000
Accounts Receivable		405,000
Inventory		632,400
Prepaid Expenses		77,760
Property, Plant & Equipment	$918,800	
Accumulated Depreciation	(78,220)	840,580
Total Assets		$2,198,740
Accounts Payable		
Inventory	$210,800	
Operating Expenses	58,320	$ 269,120
Accrued Expenses		
Operations	$116,640	
Interest	13,750	130,390
Income Tax Payable		10,200
Short-Term Notes Payable		300,000
Long-Term Notes Payable		525,000
Owners' Equity		
Capital Stock	$766,030	
Retained Earnings	198,000	964,030
Total Liabilities & Owners' Equity		$2,198,740

CASH FLOW STATEMENT FOR FIRST YEAR

Cash Flows from Operating Activities		
Net Income	$198,000	
Accounts Receivable Increase	(405,000)	
Inventory Increase	(632,400)	
Prepaid Expenses Increase	(77,760)	
Depreciation Expense	78,220	
Accounts Payable Increase	269,120	
Accrued Expenses Increase	130,390	
Income Tax Payable Increase	10,200	($ 429,230)
Cash Flows from Investing Activities		
Purchases of Property, Plant & Equipment		(918,800)
Cash Flows from Financing Activities		
Short-Term Borrowings	$300,000	
Long-Term Borrowings	525,000	
Capital Stock Issue	766,030	
Cash Dividends to Stockholders	0	1,591,030
Net Increase in Cash During Year		$ 243,000

12

INCOME TAX EXPENSE

↓

INCOME TAX PAYABLE

Refer to the connection in Exhibit D—Chapter 12 between Income Tax Expense in the Income Statement with Income Tax Payable in the Balance Sheet.

The business in our example is incorporated. A corporation, being a separate entity (person) in the eyes of the law, has several legal advantages. However, profit-motivated business corporations have one serious disadvantage—they are subject to federal and state income taxes as a separate entity.

The term "subject to" here is used deliberately. First, a corporation must earn a taxable income to be taxed. Second, there are many provisions and options in the tax laws that result in paying less tax, or perhaps no income tax at all in a given year.

It takes hundreds of pages in the federal law to define *taxable income*. Then it takes many more pages to define how to compute the income tax owed on the amount of taxable income. The 1986 Tax Reform Act, for one thing, reinforced the rules regarding the Alternative Minimum Tax (AMT) to better control the avoidance of income tax. Surely you know how complex is the federal income tax on business corporations (as well as individuals). Also, most states impose an income tax on corporations doing business in their boundaries.

This is not the place to explain taxation of business profit. To simplify, therefore, two key assumptions are made in this example.

First Simplifying Assumption

The company's accounting methods used to determine its annual taxable income are the same methods used to prepare its financial statements. There are no differences in recording its sales revenue and no differences in recording its expenses. Also, it is assumed that all recorded expenses are fully deductible for income tax purposes. Generally speaking, this harmony of income tax and financial statement accounting methods is true. Yet, many differences are permitted. To minimize its taxable income a corporation may use more conservative accounting methods in its tax returns than in its financial statements. This would lead us into very technical and complex detours from the main discussion.

Second Simplifying Assumption

In this example the federal income rate is a flat 34%, and there is no state income tax. This avoids several tax computation steps. For instance, reduced federal tax rates apply on the taxable income layers below $100,001; and, state tax is deductible for federal purposes and federal tax is deductible for state purposes.

Given these two assumptions, the corporation's taxable income is $300,000 (see Exhibit D—Chapter 12), and its total income tax for the year is:

$$
\begin{array}{lll}
\$300,000 & \times\ 34\% & =\ \$102,000 \\
\text{Taxable Income} & \text{Federal Income} & \text{Income Tax Expense} \\
& \text{Tax Rate} & \text{for year}
\end{array}
$$

Corporations have to make progress payments on their income tax as they go through the year. Simply speaking, at the start of the year a corporation makes an estimate of what its taxable income will be for the coming year. Based on this estimated taxable income, the corporation estimates its income tax for the year. The corporation has to make installment payments during the year, totaling 90% of its estimated tax for the year.

If less than 90% is paid during the year, penalties on the amount of underpayment may be imposed. However, there are several technical provisions and exceptions that may come into play such that the business escapes any penalty. It is not unrealistic to assume that a business paid in less than 90% during the year. However, we'll assume that the business in this example paid 90% and thus 10% is still owed to the Internal Revenue Service at year-end:

$102,000   × 10% balance   = $10,200
Income Tax   owed on total   Income Tax
Expense for year   income tax for   Payable
                    the year

See the connection in Exhibit D.

EXHIBIT D—CHAPTER 13

INCOME STATEMENT FOR FIRST YEAR		
Sales Revenue		$4,212,000
Cost of Goods Sold Expense		2,740,400
Gross Margin		$1,471,600
Operating Expenses	$1,010,880	
Depreciation Expense	78,220	1,089,100
Operating Earnings		$ 382,500
Interest Expense		82,500
Earnings Before Income Tax		$ 300,000
Income Tax Expense		102,000
Net Income		$ 198,000

BALANCE SHEET AT END OF FIRST YEAR		
Cash		$ 243,000
Accounts Receivable		405,000
Inventory		632,400
Prepaid Expenses		77,760
Property, Plant & Equipment	$918,800	
Accumulated Depreciation	(78,220)	840,580
Total Assets		$2,198,740
Accounts Payable		
Inventory	$210,800	
Operating Expenses	58,320	$ 269,120
Accrued Expenses		
Operations	$116,640	
Interest	13,750	130,390
Income Tax Payable		10,200
Short-Term Notes Payable		300,000
Long-Term Notes Payable		525,000
Owners' Equity		
Capital Stock	$766,030	
Retained Earnings	198,000	964,030
Total Liabilities & Owners' Equity		$2,198,740

CASH FLOW STATEMENT FOR FIRST YEAR		
Cash Flows from Operating Activities		
Net Income	$198,000	
Accounts Receivable Increase	(405,000)	
Inventory Increase	(632,400)	
Prepaid Expenses Increase	(77,760)	
Depreciation Expense	78,220	
Accounts Payable Increase	269,120	
Accrued Expenses Increase	130,390	
Income Tax Payable Increase	10,200	($ 429,230)
Cash Flows from Investing Activities		
Purchases of Property, Plant & Equipment		(918,800)
Cash Flows from Financing Activities		
Short-Term Borrowings	$300,000	
Long-Term Borrowings	525,000	
Capital Stock Issue	766,030	
Cash Dividends to Stockholders	0	1,591,030
Net Increase in Cash During Year		$ 243,000

13

NET INCOME (PROFIT)

↓

RETAINED EARNINGS

See the connection in Exhibit D—Chapter 13 linking Net Income from the Income Statement to Retained Earnings in the Balance Sheet. Net Income increases the balance in the Retained Earnings account. As explained before, but worth repeating here, net income is the final profit after deducting all expenses from sales revenue.

Now a very important question: At year-end where is net income? The answer to this question requires that we build on the discussion in previous chapters. Sales revenue results in asset increases, and expenses result in asset decreases or liability increases. Sales revenue and expenses affect virtually all the assets and most of the liabilities of a business, as explained in previous chapters.

Exhibit E presents a summary of the increases and decreases of the company's assets and liabilities resulting from its sales revenue and expenses for the year. The amounts of these increases and decreases are precisely the main points discussed in earlier chapters, except for the decrease of Cash. The cash flow analysis of net income is extremely important to business managers, creditors, and investors, and is discussed fully in the next chapter. For now you might refer to the earlier discussion in Chapter 1 (page 5) which shows the summary of cash receipts from sales and cash disbursements for expenses. Notice that the bottom line of that cash flow summary is a $429,230 decrease in Cash; in Exhibit E Cash also shows a $429,230 decrease.

EXHIBIT E—ASSET AND LIABILITY CHANGES CAUSED BY NET INCOME (OPERATING) ACTIVITIES

Asset Changes		
Cash	−$429,230	
Accounts Receivable	+ 405,000	
Inventory	+ 632,400	
Prepaid Expenses	+ 77,760	
Property, Plant & Equipment	− 78,220	
Total Asset Increases		$607,710
Liability Changes		
Accounts Payable	+$269,120	
Accrued Expenses	+ 130,390	
Income Tax Payable	+ 10,200	
Total Liability Increases		409,710
Net Income (Asset Increases less Liability Increases)		$198,000

The main point here is that net income consists of a mix of increases and decreases in several asset and liability accounts—as shown in Exhibit E. Net income is not simply money in the bank. In fact cash decreased during the first year from the company's net income-making operations.

Dividends, if and when paid, are recorded as decreases in Retained Earnings. But because of the cash decrease from net income, the company did not distribute any cash dividends to its stockholders. Thus Retained Earnings increased by the entire $198,000 amount of net income. (See the line of connection in Exhibit D, which indicates that no cash dividends were paid.)

In short, the balance in Retained Earnings is just that—the amount of net income earned *and* retained by the business. Sometimes it's called Undistributed Net Income, or Undistributed Earnings, though the title Retained Earnings is much more common.*

It's very important to understand that Retained Earnings is *not* an asset. Nor does it indicate how much cash or how much of any other particular asset the company has. Think of Retained Earnings as a balance account, the last weight you put on the scales to make for a perfect balance.

Let's return to Exhibit E again, which summarizes the asset and liability changes from net income for the year. To summarize even further, net income can be put as follows:

$607,710   − $409,710   = $198,000
Increases in assets   Increases in liabilities   Net income

* God forbid, but occasionally you still see the term "Earned Surplus" (instead of Retained Earnings). This title is especially confusing and as outmoded as the Model T.

Without Retained Earnings in the Balance Sheet, net income would cause an imbalance, like a teeter-totter out of balance:

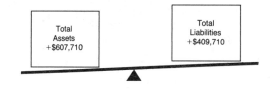

With Retained Earnings there is a balance:

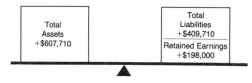

Retained Earnings does more than keep the Balance Sheet in a condition of equality. It keeps track of how much of total owners' (stockholders') equity was earned and retained by the business versus how much capital has been invested from time to time by the owners (which is recorded in the other owners' equity account). Legally these two sources of owners' equity must be separated.

Looking at the Retained Earnings balance is like looking into a mirror. The real profit earned by a business is found in the assets less the liabilities of the business. Retained Earnings is only the image in the mirror (in one amount).

EXHIBIT D—CHAPTER 14

INCOME STATEMENT FOR FIRST YEAR

Sales Revenue		$4,212,000
Cost of Goods Sold Expense		2,740,400
Gross Margin		$1,471,600
Operating Expenses	$1,010,880	
Depreciation Expense	78,220	1,089,100
Operating Earnings		$ 382,500
Interest Expense		82,500
Earnings Before Income Tax		$ 300,000
Income Tax Expense		102,000
Net Income		$ 198,000

BALANCE SHEET AT END OF FIRST YEAR

Cash		$ 243,000
Accounts Receivable		405,000
Inventory		632,400
Prepaid Expenses		77,760
Property, Plant & Equipment	$918,800	
Accumulated Depreciation	(78,220)	840,580
Total Assets		$2,198,740
Accounts Payable		
Inventory	$210,800	
Operating Expenses	58,320	$ 269,120
Accrued Expenses		
Operations	$116,640	
Interest	13,750	130,390
Income Tax Payable		10,200
Short-Term Notes Payable		300,000
Long-Term Notes Payable		525,000
Owners' Equity		
Capital Stock	$766,030	
Retained Earnings	198,000	964,030
Total Liabilities & Owners' Equity		$2,198,740

CASH FLOW STATEMENT FOR FIRST YEAR

Cash Flows from Operating Activities

Net Income	$198,000	
Accounts Receivable Increase	(405,000)	
Inventory Increase	(632,400)	
Prepaid Expenses Increase	(77,760)	
Depreciation Expense	78,220	
Accounts Payable Increase	269,120	
Accrued Expenses Increase	130,390	
Income Tax Payable Increase	10,200	($ 429,230)

Cash Flows from Investing Activities

Purchases of Property, Plant & Equipment		(918,800)

Cash Flows from Financing Activities

Short-Term Borrowings	$300,000	
Long-Term Borrowings	525,000	
Capital Stock Issue	766,030	
Cash Dividends to Stockholders	0	1,591,030
Net Increase in Cash During Year		$ 243,000

14

CASH FLOW ANALYSIS OF PROFIT

Making sales and controlling expenses is a demanding task, to say the least. However, earning an adequate profit is not enough. Managing cash is just as important. Enough cash must be available *when needed*. Earning a good profit does not necessarily guarantee an adequate cash flow when needed.

In short, business managers have a double duty: to earn profit, and to convert the profit into cash reasonably soon. Waiting too long to turn profit into cash reduces the value of the profit because of the time value of money.

Managers use the Income Statement to review and evaluate profit performance and to prepare the profit plan for the coming year. Likewise, managers should use the *Cash Flow Statement* to review cash flows for the year just ended and to prepare the cash flow budget for the coming year. Not to plan cash flows would invite disaster.

Exhibit D—Chapter 14 presents the company's Cash Flow Statement for its first year of business on the right side of its Balance Sheet. The enclosed area of the Cash Flow Statement is discussed in this chapter, and the remainder of the statement is discussed in Chapter 16.

The company's Cash Flow Statement begins with an analysis of the cash flow effects from operations, which are all those activities directly a part of making profit (net income). In other words, operations refers to those transactions involved in making sales and incurring expenses.

Net income is earned when sales revenue and expenses are recorded. These recordings, in large part, are made either before or after the related cash flows occur. Over a long time, say 10 to 15 years, the total increase in cash would be very close to the total net income earned. But in any one year the cash flow can be considerably less or more than the amount of net income reported in the Income Statement for that year.

Changes in a company's operating assets and operating liabilities during the year usually cause cash flow from operations (profit) to be quite different from net income for the year—which is certainly true in this case! Please note in Exhibit D the lines extending from the operating assets and operating liabilities into the Cash Flow Statement.

Accounts Receivable increased during the year, which means that $405,000 of its sales revenue for the year had not been received in cash by year-end. Only $3,807,000 of the company's sales revenue was actually collected in cash ($4,212,000 sales revenue less $405,000 Accounts Receivable = $3,807,000 cash received). So the $405,000 increase in Accounts Receivable during the year is deducted from net income.

Next, Inventory increased $632,400 during the year. In addition to its cost of goods sold during the year, the company made inventory purchases of $632,400 to build up its stock of goods held for sale. These purchases have to be paid for, of course. The $632,400 is an additional demand on cash, so it is deducted from net income. (Part of the inventory purchases are still unpaid at year-end; the Accounts Payable for these are considered later.)

Prepaid Expenses increased $77,760 during the year. In addition to its operating expenses, the company had to prepay $77,760 of next year's expenses, which is the ending balance of Prepaid Expenses. This $77,760 is an additional demand on cash during the year, and thus is deducted from net income.

To this point, things look pretty bad. Over one million dollars has been deducted from net income. However, on the other side of the coin as it were, the company did not have to pay out in cash the entire amount of expenses reported in the Income Statement. These unpaid expenses are next shown in the Cash Flow Statement.

First of all, depreciation expense is not a cash outlay. See Exhibit D again. Notice that the depreciation expense increases the Accumulated Depreciation account, which is deducted from the Property, Plant & Equipment asset account. This asset account, not Cash, is decreased. So, depreciation is added to net income.*

The earlier chapters explain that three liabilities are directly affected by the expenses of the business—Accounts Payable, Accrued Expenses, and Income Tax Payable. An increase in an operating liability during the year means that cash was not paid out by the amount of the increase.

The increases for each liability are their year-end balances because this example is for the first year of business. (There were no liabilities at the start of the year.) The year-end balances are the unpaid amounts resulting from the expenses during the year. Cash payments of these amounts were avoided during the year; cash will not be paid until next year. Thus, each increase is added to net income—see Exhibit D again.

To sum up: Starting with $198,000 net income, deducting the three negative cash flow factors, and adding the four positive cash flow factors, gives the *negative* $429,230 cash flow from operations—see Exhibit D once again.

This $429,230 cash *outflow* during the first year from net income activities required that the company borrow money and raise capital from its stockholders to cover the "pull down" on cash from its profit-making operations. Sources of capital are discussed in Chapter 16.

Such a large negative impact on cash from earning net income is a one-time first year start-up situation. Recall that the example is for the company's first year of business. In later years net income usually generates an increase in cash, although not usually equal to or even very close to the amount of net income. Chapter 17 presents the cash flow analysis from net income for the company's second year of business. There is a healthy cash inflow in the second year.

* You may see a figure called "cash flow from net income" that is simply the net income amount plus the depreciation expense for the period. But this is not really cash flow from operations. Cash flow analysis must look at all the assets and liabilities affected by sales revenue and expenses.

EXHIBIT D—CHAPTER 15

INCOME STATEMENT FOR FIRST YEAR

Sales Revenue		$4,212,000
Cost of Goods Sold Expense		2,740,400
Gross Margin		$1,471,600
Operating Expenses	$1,010,880	
Depreciation Expense	78,220	1,089,100
Operating Earnings		$ 382,500
Interest Expense		82,500
Earnings Before Income Tax		$ 300,000
Income Tax Expense		102,000
Net Income		$ 198,000

BALANCE SHEET AT END OF FIRST YEAR

Cash		$ 243,000
Accounts Receivable		405,000
Inventory		632,400
Prepaid Expenses		77,760
Property, Plant & Equipment	$918,800	
Accumulated Depreciation	(78,220)	840,580
Total Assets		$2,198,740
Accounts Payable		
Inventory	$210,800	
Operating Expenses	58,320	$ 269,120
Accrued Expenses		
Operations	$116,640	
Interest	13,750	130,390
Income Tax Payable		10,200
Short-Term Notes Payable		300,000
Long-Term Notes Payable		525,000
Owners' Equity		
Capital Stock	$766,030	
Retained Earnings	198,000	964,030
Total Liabilities & Owners' Equity		$2,198,740

CASH FLOW STATEMENT FOR FIRST YEAR

Cash Flows from Operating Activities

Cash Receipts from Sales	$3,807,000	
Cash Payments for Products	(3,162,000)	
Cash Payments for Operating Expenses	(913,680)	
Cash Payments for Interest	(68,750)	
Cash Payments for Income Tax	91,800	
		($429,230)

Cash Flows from Investing Activities

Purchases of Property, Plant & Equipment		(918,800)

Cash Flows from Financing Activities

Short-Term Borrowings	$300,000	
Long-Term Borrowings	525,000	
Capital Stock Issue	766,030	
Cash Dividends to Stockholders	0	1,591,030
Net Increase in Cash During Year		$ 243,000

15

ALTERNATIVE FORMAT FOR REPORTING CASH FLOW FROM PROFIT

Two Formats

I have a minor confession to make here. The format of the Cash Flow Statement in Exhibit D—first introduced in Chapter 3 and continued through Chapter 14—is *not* the only acceptable format for this primary financial statement. It's the one I like best. For one thing this format starts with net income from the Income Statement, which is the natural stepping stone between the two statements. Equally important, the format ties in with assets and liabilities from the Balance Sheet. I definitely favor this format for its value in explaining how the three primary financial statements are connected with each other. However, you'll also see another, quite different format for the Cash Flow Statement.

In its recent (November 1987) authoritative pronouncement on reporting cash flows, the Financial Accounting Standards Board (FASB) decided that two formats are acceptable. I don't know why the FASB didn't choose just one format, so that all companies would report cash flows the same way. But they didn't.

There are many issues in financial accounting for which you can make good arguments for two (or more) different methods. For example, in later chapters we'll look into the problems of measuring cost of goods sold expense and depreciation expense. For both these expenses there are alternative but equally acceptable methods of accounting. Cash flow reporting is another example; either one of two formats is acceptable—the one shown earlier, which has been explained in Chapter 14, *or* the second one explained in this chapter.

If you're the chief executive of a business you should choose the format that best serves your company's management needs. As an "outside" creditor or investor you have to understand both formats, since you'll see both in financial reports. It's hard to predict which one will become more popular.

The Direct Method Format

Please examine the Cash Flow Statement in Exhibit D on page 72. Notice in particular the first section of the statement, *Cash Flows from Operating Activities*, which is highlighted. This part of the statement is different than before, very different I might add. This format reports the summary of cash receipts and payments of the profit-making-operations (activities) of the business. This format is called the *direct method*, whereas the earlier format is called the *indirect method*.

Don't ask me where the FASB got these names. I would have called the earlier format the "comparative balance sheet" format; it builds on changes in the balance sheet accounts, which to me is the natural and direct method of presenting the Cash Flow Statement. (Our example is for the first year of business, so the ending balances of assets and liabilities are also the amount of changes for the year.) I would have called the second format the "cash flows summary" format, but the FASB decided to call it the direct method.

Notice immediately that cash flow from profit (operating activities) is exactly the same amount as before. To make sure of this, compare the *negative* $429,230 cash flow from operating activities in Exhibit D on page 72 with the earlier format on page 68. Both formats arrive at the same number, though the manner of presentation is quite different.

Also notice that the other two sections of the Cash Flow Statement are the same. In other words, the cash flows from investing activities and from financing activities are the same for both formats—only the cash flows from operating activities section is different. The other two sections of the Cash Flow Statement are discussed in the following chapter.

The direct method format starts with total cash receipts from customers for the year. In our example this amount is $3,807,000, which does *not* include the amount of Accounts Receivable at year-end. Next, the total of cash payments for products is deducted—see the $3,162,000 figure in Exhibit D (page 72). This is the total amount paid out for inventory purchases (or manufacturing costs) during the year, including the amount of inventory still on hand at year-end that hasn't been sold yet.

The next item is the total amount of cash payments for operating expenses during the year ($913,680). This amount includes a relatively small amount for expenses that are prepaid at the end of the year, but does not include expenses unpaid at year-end that are recorded either as an Accounts Payable or Accrued Expenses liability. No depreciation expense is included in the direct method format, because depreciation is not a cash outlay. The interest expense cash payment ($68,750) does not include the unpaid amount of interest expense at year-end. Likewise, the income tax cash payment ($91,800) does not include the unpaid amount of income tax expense at year-end.

Reconciling the Cash Basis and Accrual Basis

Basically, the direct method format presents a "cash basis" Income Statement. By now I hope that I have made very clear that the Income Statement is reported on the *accrual basis of accounting*, which is absolutely necessary for measuring sales revenue and expenses to determine the profit (net income) of a business. The company in our example earned profit (net income) of $198,000—see its Income Statement in Exhibit D. It did *not* suffer a loss of $429,230, which is the "bottom line" of the cash flows summary of its revenue and expenses.

The distinction between the cash basis and accrual basis is extraordinarily important. Exhibit F on the next page explains the differences between the cash basis and the accrual basis for our example.

The $405,000 year-end balance of Accounts Receivable, being the amount of sales not yet collected by year-end, is added to the total $3,807,000 cash receipts from customers to determine the $4,212,000 sales revenue for the year on the accrual basis.

The $3,162,000 total cash payments for products during the year is too much to charge to Cost of Goods Sold Expense. Some products were not sold by year-end, which are in the company's ending inventory. Ending inventory also includes company's ending inventory. Ending inventory also includes products not yet paid for by year-end, the amount of which is found in Accounts Payable—Inventory. Notice in Exhibit F that ending inventory is deducted but Accounts Payable for inventory is added to the cash flow amount to arrive at the $2,740,400 Cost of Goods Sold Expense on the accrual basis.

During the year the company paid $913,680 for its various operating expenses. Of this total amount $77,760 went for certain expenses that are prepaid at year-end, so this amount should be subtracted from the cash payment total to get the correct (accrual basis) amount of operating expenses for the year. On the other side, the company had not paid for all its operating expenses by the end of the year. There were $58,320 of unpaid operating expenses in Accounts Payable—Operating Expenses at year-end and another $116,640 in Accrued Expenses at year-end. As you can see in Exhibit F, the amount of prepaid expenses is deducted and the two liabilities are added to the cash flow amount, which leads over to $1,010,880 Operating Expenses on the accrual basis.

Depreciation is not a cash outlay; thus, in the Cash Flows column a zero is entered in Exhibit F. But as explained earlier Depreciation Expense must be recorded. Depreciation of $78,220

EXHIBIT F—CASH FLOWS RECONCILED WITH ACCRUAL BASIS OF NET INCOME (for First Year of Business)

Cash Flows			Differences and Brief Explanation	Accrual Basis
Sales	$3,807,000	+$405,000	Accounts Receivable (sales were made this period even though cash will not be collected until next period)	$4,212,000
Goods sold	(3,162,000)	− 632,400	Inventory (goods have not been sold yet but will be next period)	
		+ 210,800	Accounts Payable (goods have been purchased but not paid for by end of year)	(2,740,400)
Operating expenses	(913,680)	− 77,760	Prepaid Expenses (costs paid for that will benefit next period)	
		+ 58,320	Accounts Payable (costs that benefited this period but will not be paid until next period)	
		+ 116,640	Accrued Expenses (estimated amount of accumulated costs that benefited this period but won't be paid until next period)	(1,010,880)
Depreciation	-0-	+ 78,220	Accumulated Depreciation (decrease in long-lived operating assets to recognize using the resources during this period)	(78,220)
Interest	(68,750)	+ 13,750	Accrued Expenses (unpaid interest at year-end for the use of debt during this period)	(82,500)
Income tax	(91,800)	+ 10,200	Income Tax Payable (unpaid amount owed on the taxable income earned this period)	(102,000)
Cash Decrease from Operations	($ 429,230)		Net Income	$ 198,000

is recorded in the first year of business, which is included in the accrual basis.

The company paid most but not all of its interest and income tax expenses for the year. Notice in Exhibit F that the amounts unpaid at year-end, which are in Accrued Expenses—Interest and Income Tax Payable, are added to the cash flow amounts to get over to the accrual basis amounts for these two expenses.

In short, even though the net cash flow from its operating activities (sales revenue and expenses) was a negative $429,230 for the year, on the accrual basis the company earned profit (net income) of $198,000. Please see Exhibit F again.

As you may have surmised, companies are not required to report a "Schedule F" type of reconciliation in their external financial statements. I doubt that any will. Yet, the reconciliation of the cash basis and accrual basis is extraordinarily important to understand. One of the reasons I like the indirect method format (explained in the preceding chapter) is that the adjustments to net income leave a clear trail of reconciliation to the cash flow from net income, and also tie in with the changes in the Balance Sheet accounts.

Exhibit F is also useful for another purpose—to focus attention on the key assumptions we make in accounting for profit on the accrual basis. For instance, we assume that all accounts receivable will be collected. We assume that all inventory will be sold at normal prices. We assume that the business will continue in operation to take advantage of its prepaid expenses and its fixed assets. We assume that the accounts payable, accrued expenses, and income tax will be paid at the amounts recorded.

If any of these assumptions are subject to doubt, profit measurement becomes more of a problem. For example, not all the accounts receivable may be collected. So, we should allow for bad debts expense. Some of the inventory may never be sold or may have to be sold at greatly reduced prices. So, we should write down inventory to record its loss of value. Such accounting problems are the next step in learning financial statement accounting, which go beyond the scope of this book.

INCOME STATEMENT FOR FIRST YEAR

Sales Revenue		$4,212,000
Cost of Goods Sold Expense		2,740,400
Gross Margin		$1,471,600
Operating Expenses	$1,010,880	
Depreciation Expense	78,220	1,089,100
Operating Earnings		$ 382,500
Interest Expense		82,500
Earnings Before Income Tax		$ 300,000
Income Tax Expense		102,000
Net Income		$ 198,000

BALANCE SHEET AT END OF FIRST YEAR

Cash		$ 243,000
Accounts Receivable		405,000
Inventory		632,400
Prepaid Expenses		77,760
Property, Plant & Equipment	$918,800	
Accumulated Depreciation	(78,220)	840,580
Total Assets		$2,198,740
Accounts Payable		
Inventory	$210,800	
Operating Expenses	58,320	$ 269,120
Accrued Expenses		
Operations	$116,640	
Interest	13,750	130,390
Income Tax Payable		10,200
Short-Term Notes Payable		300,000
Long-Term Notes Payable		525,000
Owners' Equity		
Capital Stock	$766,030	
Retained Earnings	198,000	964,030
Total Liabilities & Owners' Equity		$2,198,740

CASH FLOW STATEMENT FOR FIRST YEAR

Cash Flows from Operating Activities		
Net Income	$198,000	
Accounts Receivable Increase	(405,000)	
Inventory Increase	(632,400)	
Prepaid Expenses Increase	(77,760)	
Depreciation Expense	78,220	
Accounts Payable Increase	269,120	
Accrued Expenses Increase	130,390	
Income Tax Payable Increase	10,200	($ 429,230)
Cash Flows from Investing Activities		
Purchases of Property, Plant & Equipment		(918,800)
Cash Flows from Financing Activities		
Short-Term Borrowings	$300,000	
Long-Term Borrowings	525,000	
Capital Stock Issue	766,030	
Cash Dividends to Stockholders	0	1,591,030
Net Increase in Cash During Year		$ 243,000

16

OTHER CASH FLOWS: FINANCING AND INVESTING ACTIVITIES

During the first year of business the company had to build its accounts receivable, inventory, and prepaid expenses from a zero base at the start of the year to their year-end balances. Also, the company needed to build a cash balance. Inventory was financed partly from an increase in accounts payable. Otherwise the capital invested in these assets had to come from other sources.

Obviously the company had to raise a good deal of capital. The remainder of the Cash Flow Statement reports the sources of capital raised during the year, and the uses of this capital. Please refer to Exhibit D—Chapter 16. In particular, notice the last two sections of the statement: (1) Cash Flows from Investing Activities; and (2) Cash Flows from Financing Activities.

The company borrowed $825,000—$300,000 on short-term notes and $525,000 on long-term notes. (Some of the short-term notes, having maturities of less than one year, were paid and replaced by new short-term notes during the year, but this turnover needn't concern us.) In addition the stockholders invested $766,030 at the start of the year, for which they received stock shares from the corporation. Together the debt and equity sources of capital provided $1,591,030. These sources of capital are reported in the Cash Flows from Financing Activities section in the Cash Flow Statement. Refer to Exhibit D on page 80 again.

Decisions on how to finance a business, concerning the mix of equity (stock), short-term debt, long-term debt, and other types of securities are financial management policy issues, not accounting matters as such. Needless to say, many factors and alternatives have to be considered, which are far beyond the scope of this book.

The company used $918,800 of the total capital to purchase various long-lived operating assets (fixed assets), leaving $672,230 for other purposes. The preceding two chapters explain that the profit-making activities of the business were not a source of cash during the year. Instead, the operating activities required the *use* of $429,230 of cash.

Subtracting this $429,230 negative cash flow from profit from the $672,230 of capital available after the fixed assets were purchased leaves $243,000. The company could have paid cash dividends to its stockholders, but did not. Hence, $243,000 is the cash balance at year-end. Look at Exhibit D again; notice the ending cash balance is $243,000.

Is this cash balance too much? Too little? Should the company have paid at least some cash dividends to its stockholders? The ending cash balance equals 3 weeks of annual sales revenue: [$4,212,000 Sales Revenue ÷ 52 weeks = $81,000 per week; $81,000 × 3 = $243,000].

The company earned $198,000 net income for the year. A cash dividend of, say, $81,000 could have been paid, which seems reasonable relative to the net income. But, this would have left the company with an ending cash balance equal to only 2 weeks of its annual sales revenue.

Is 2 weeks too small for a working cash balance? Does prudence demand at least 3 weeks? Companies differ widely on the basic question regarding their working cash balances. There's no standard practice, to say the least. What if it were *your* business? What would be your target for a normal working cash balance? This is one of the basic questions of business finance, which goes beyond the scope of this book.

At this point please follow each line of connection in Exhibit D from the investing and financing activities sections of the Cash Flow Statement to its destination in the Balance Sheet. We have accounted for all the sources and uses of cash during the year. And, all the items in the Balance Sheet have been explained.

In summary, the Cash Flow Statement deserves as much attention and study as the Income Statement and Balance Sheet. Cash flows affect the ability of the company to pay its debts on time and to pay cash dividends from net income; and, adequate cash sources are needed for making investments in operating assets. Creditors and investors are, or should be, as interested in cash flows as managers.

17

GROWTH VERSUS NO-GROWTH: IMPACT ON CASH FLOW

In previous chapters we've analyzed the company's financial statements for its first, or start-up, year of business. The first year is the natural starting point for introducing financial statements, which also brings out the special cash flow demands during the first year. Once over the first-year hump, however, managing cash flow and financial condition takes on a different character.

In analyzing cash flow from operations for the first year of business we concentrated on end-of-year effects. For example, Accounts Receivable was $405,000 at the end of the first year; this means total cash receipts from customers were this much less than sales revenue for the first year. In the second year of business (and succeeding years) we must consider beginning-of-year effects also. For example, the $405,000 Accounts Receivable at the end of the first year carries forward as the beginning balance at the start of the second year. The $405,000 is collected during the second year, which adds to cash inflow in year two.

In summary, *both ending and beginning* balances of every asset and every liability affected by sales revenue and expenses have to be considered in determining the cash flow from operations in a continuing year of business (every year after the first year).

Beginning balances, compared with ending balances, have *reverse* effects on cash flow. If the ending balance has a negative effect, the beginning balance has a positive effect—and vice versa. If the ending balance happened to equal the beginning balance there would be a break-even effect. For instance, if the Accounts Receivable ending balance were the same as its beginning balance, cash receipts from customers during the year would be the same as sales revenue for the year.

The No-Growth Case:
A Very Useful Point of Reference

A very useful baseline of reference for understanding the reverse effects between beginning and ending balances is the no-growth case. Exhibit G on the next page shows the company's financial statements for its second year of business, in exactly the same format as before, on the assumption that sales revenue and all expenses are exactly the same as in the first year.

In essence, we're assuming no inflation and no changes in the quantity of goods sold or the "quantities" of all expenses (e.g., number of hours worked by employees, number of kilowatts of electricity used, etc.). Of course, this no-growth, or steady-state assumption is not very realistic. But before we look at the growth case, the no-growth financial statements reveal several valuable points about what happens to cash flow from operations and the financial condition of the business.

In Exhibit G the Income Statement for year two is an exact duplicate of year one. The Balance Sheet at the end of year two is mostly the same as a year ago, with a few important changes to be discussed. But look at the Cash Flow Statement; what a difference from the first year!

Cash *inflow* from operations in year two is $276,220, compared with $429,230 cash *outflow* in year one. The reason for this huge difference, even though sales revenue and expenses are the same both years, is that the company started the second year with sufficient amounts of the current assets and current liabilities required by the sales revenue and expenses, and none increased during the second year. The ending balances are all equal to the beginning balances. Because of the reverse effects of ending and beginning balances, there is a break-even (or zero) effect on cash flow from operations in the year. See the Cash Flow Statement in Exhibit G.

In other words, in the no-growth situation a company does not have to increase its Accounts Receivable, Inventory, or Prepaid Expenses. In rough terms, the beginning balances are converted into cash during the year and this cash provides the ending balances, which are the same amounts.

Also, in the no-growth situation a company does not increase its Accounts Payable, Accrued Expenses, or Income Tax Payable. In rough terms, the beginning balances are paid during the year but the ending balances are not paid during the year. The beginning and ending balances of these liabilities are the same amounts; so the "payoff" of the beginning balances is offset with an equal amount of "borrowing" in the form of the ending balances.

One other asset is affected in recording expenses for the

EXHIBIT G—NO-GROWTH CASE FOR SECOND YEAR

INCOME STATEMENT FOR SECOND YEAR

Sales Revenue		$4,212,000
Cost of Goods Sold Expense		2,740,400
Gross Margin		$1,471,600
Operating Expenses	$1,010,880	
Depreciation Expense	78,220	1,089,100
Operating Earnings		$ 382,500
Interest Expense		82,500
Earnings Before Income Tax		$ 300,000
Income Tax Expense		102,000
Net Income		$ 198,000

BALANCE SHEET AT END OF SECOND YEAR

Cash		$ 438,220
Accounts Receivable		405,000
Inventory		632,400
Prepaid Expenses		77,760
Property, Plant & Equipment	$918,800	
Accumulated Depreciation	(156,440)	762,360
Total Assets		$2,315,740
Accounts Payable		
Inventory	$210,800	
Operating Expenses	58,320	$ 269,120
Accrued Expenses		
Operations	116,640	
Interest	13,750	130,390
Income Tax Payable		10,200
Short-Term Notes Payable		300,000
Long-Term Notes Payable		525,000
Owners' Equity		
Capital Stock	$766,030	
Retained Earnings	315,000	1,081,030
Total Liabilities & Owners' Equity		$2,315,740

CASH FLOW STATEMENT FOR SECOND YEAR

Cash Flows from Operating Activities		
Net Income	$198,000	
Accounts Receivable Increase	0	
Inventory Increase	0	
Prepaid Expenses Increase	0	
Depreciation Expense	78,220	
Accounts Payable Increase	0	
Accrued Expenses Increase	0	
Income Tax Payable Increase	0	$276,220
Cash Flows from Investing Activities		
Purchases of Property, Plant & Equipment		0
Cash Flows from Financing Activities		
Short-Term Borrowings	0	
Long-Term Borrowings	0	
Capital Stock Issue	0	
Cash Dividends to Stockholders	(81,000)	(81,000)
Net Increase in Cash During Year		$195,220

year. The long-lived operating assets were decreased $78,220 by the depreciation expense charged to year two (see Exhibit G). Recording depreciation expense does not decrease cash. Thus the amount of depreciation expense is a positive cash flow factor (the only one!) in the Cash Flow Statement. In rough terms, the company "sold" $78,220 of its long-term assets to its customers. Sales prices were set high enough to recover $78,220 of the capital invested in the assets. In this sense, sales revenue in part reimburses the company for the use of these assets in the operations of the business.

There was a "conversion" of $78,220 out of the assets to cash during year two; depreciation can be quite properly thought of in this manner. In addition, the company earned $198,000 net income without any changes in the current assets and current liabilities affected by sales revenue and expenses. So all the net income was available in cash *and* depreciation was converted into cash. Thus cash flow from net income is $276,220 in the second year.

What happened to the $276,220? The company paid $81,000 cash dividends to its stockholders (see Exhibit G). The company did *not* replace any of its long-lived operating assets during year two. The assets were purchased new at the start of year one, and none need replacing yet. After a few years of business, however—even in a no-growth situation—the machines, equipment, and so on have to be replaced to maintain the capacity and services provided by the assets.

There were no stock issues and no increases in debt during year two. Therefore, the $276,220 cash inflow from net income (operations) less the $81,000 cash dividends gives a $195,220 increase in Cash (see Exhibit G). Cash started the year with a $243,000 balance, so its balance at the end of year two is $438,220.

Also, note that Retained Earnings increased $117,000 during the second year ($198,000 net income less $81,000 dividends), so its balance at the end of year two is $315,000 ($198,000 balance at end of year one plus the $117,000 increase during the second year). What else? Oh, you might also note that the Accumulated Depreciation account now has two years of depreciation expense in it.

The Growth Case: Impacts on Cash Flow

Growth is the central strategy of most businesses. The good news is that growth should increase net income. The bad news is that growth puts strains on cash flow. The greater the growth, the heavier the strains on cash flow.

Instead of a no-growth situation, suppose the company's sales revenue increased 20% in its second year of business. On pages 92 and 93 Exhibit H presents the company's *comparative* financial statements for its first and second year of business.

Comparative data can be reported in different ways. In Exhibit H the Income Statement reports *percent* changes and the Balance Sheet reports *dollar amounts* of changes, whereas the Cash Flow Statement does *not* report changes. Unfortunately most corporations do *not* report changes in their comparative financial statements, which puts the burden on readers of their financial statements to calculate the percents or dollar amounts of changes.

In this example the company's Cost of Goods Sold Expense also increased 20%, exactly the same as the increase in Sales Revenue. Thus, its Gross Margin increased 20% as well. Notice the first three lines in the comparative Income Statement show

20% increases. The next line, Operating Expenses, increased only 16%—considerably less than 20%. Not all operating expenses moved in lock-step with sales revenue. Some expenses result in *economies of scale* on a larger sales base. The business gains more efficiency or higher productivity from some expenses, so these expenses do not increase proportionally as much as sales revenue.

Next is Depreciation Expense. Depreciation is based on the cost of Property, Plant & Equipment, the company's long-term fixed assets. At this point, therefore, the question is whether the company had to increase its fixed assets to support the 20% sales revenue growth. Generally speaking companies don't operate at full capacity, which means they are not making 100% use of their fixed assets. Some sales growth—usually at least 10%, perhaps even 20% or more—can be taken on without expanding their fixed assets. But it's difficult to generalize from company to company.

Fixed assets are capital investment decisions having a long-term planning horizon. Often companies expand their fixed asset base not just for the coming year, but for two years or longer. In this example the company made a major increase in its fixed assets during year two, to lay the foundation for forecast sales growth over the next several years. Notice in its comparative Balance Sheet that Property, Plant & Equipment increased $415,800. Thus, its Depreciation Expense increased sharply in year two, as you can see in Exhibit H.

At this point we should look at cash flow from profit (operating activities). The company generated $220,743 from its profit-making operations during year two—see the Cash Flow Statement in Exhibit H. This is much better than its first year, as you can see. However, cash flow in the growth case is much less than in the no-growth case. The company realized over $276,000 cash flow in the no-growth case (refer to Exhibit G).

In the growth case the company had to increase its short-term operating assets, which had negative impacts on cash flow. On the other hand, increases in its operating liabilities benefited cash flow from profit. But the final result is that cash flow is less than the net income for the year, which is the typical result of growth.

To finance the major expansion of its fixed assets the company increased its short-term and long-term debt, which in turn caused higher interest expense in year two. Did the company borrow too much? Much depends on the company's cash balance policy. Notice the company's balance of Cash at the end of year two is $347,943, which equals about 3½ weeks of sales revenue for the year. Many companies would consider this much working cash balance more than adequate.

The company decided not to pay a cash dividend, as you can see in its Cash Flow Statement. Perhaps the company should have paid a cash dividend of, say, $100,000, although this would have reduced its cash balance by $100,000. One main purpose of financial statement analysis is to identify financial policy decisions of this sort.

One final comment: explosive growth can cause *negative* cash flow from profit. In our example sales revenue increased 20% in year two, which is fairly substantial. Suppose sales revenue had doubled—rather fantastic growth to say the least. Assuming that the basic relationships of its operating assets and liabilities to its sales revenue and expenses held the same, the company's cash flow from profit in year two would be very much the same as in year one, that is, a very large *negative* cash flow. This would have demanded major increases from its sources of capital to finance such large sales growth.

EXHIBIT H—COMPARATIVE FINANCIAL STATEMENTS FOR 20% GROWTH IN SECOND YEAR

COMPARATIVE INCOME STATEMENTS

	Year One	Year Two	Change
Sales Revenue	$4,212,000	$5,054,400	+20%
Cost of Goods Sold Expense	2,740,400	3,288,480	+20
Gross Margin	$1,471,600	$1,765,920	+20
Operating Expenses	1,010,880	1,167,566	+16
Depreciation Expense	78,220	106,820	+37
Operating Earnings	$ 382,500	$ 491,534	+29
Interest Expense	82,500	100,500	+22
Earnings Before Income Tax	$ 300,000	$ 391,034	+30
Income Tax Expense	102,000	132,951	+30
Net Income	$ 198,000	$ 258,082	+30

COMPARATIVE CASH FLOW STATEMENTS

	Year One	Year Two
Cash Flows from Operating Activities		
Net Income	$ 198,000	$258,082
Accounts Receivable Increase	(405,000)	(81,000)
Inventory Increase	(632,400)	(126,480)
Prepaid Expenses Increase	(77,760)	(12,053)
Depreciation Expense	78,220	106,820
Accounts Payable Increase	269,120	51,200
Accrued Expenses Increase	130,390	21,079
Income Tax Payable Increase	10,200	3,095
Cash Flow from Profit	($ 429,230)	$220,743
Cash Flows from Investing Activities		
Purchases of Property, Plant & Equipment	($ 918,800)	($415,800)
Cash Flows from Financing Activities		
Short-Term Borrowings	$ 300,000	$100,000
Long-Term Borrowings	525,000	200,000
Capital Stock Issue	766,030	0
Cash Dividends	0	0
Net Cash from Financing	$1,591,030	$300,000
Net Increase in Cash	$ 243,000	$104,943

COMPARATIVE YEAR-END BALANCE SHEETS

	Year One		Year Two		Change
Cash		$ 243,000		$ 347,943	$104,943
Accounts Receivable		405,000		486,000	81,000
Inventory		632,400		758,880	126,480
Prepaid Expenses		77,760		89,813	12,053
Property, Plant & Equipment	$918,800		$1,334,600		415,800
Accumulated Depreciation	(78,220)		(185,040)		(106,820)
		840,580		1,149,560	
Total Assets		$2,198,740		$2,832,196	$633,456
Accounts Payable					
Inventory	$210,800		$ 252,960		
Operating Expenses	58,320	269,120	67,360	$ 320,320	$ 51,200
Accrued Expenses					
Operations	$116,640		$ 134,719		
Interest	13,750	130,390	16,750	151,469	21,079
Income Tax Payable		10,200		13,295	3,095
Short-Term Notes Payable		300,000		400,000	100,000
Long-Term Notes Payable		525,000		725,000	200,000
Owners' Equity					
Capital Stock	$766,030		$ 766,030		0
Retained Earnings	$198,000		456,082		258,082
		964,030		1,222,112	
Total Liabilities & Owners' Equity		$2,198,740		$2,832,196	$633,456

18

FOOTNOTES—THE FINE PRINT IN FINANCIAL REPORTS

Pick up any annual financial report and you'll see the Balance Sheet, Income Statement, and Cash Flow Statement. Also you'll find two pages or more of footnotes. Footnotes provide the "fine print" that goes along with the three principal financial statements.

Top-level managers should never forget that they are responsible for the financial statements and the accompanying footnotes. The footnotes are an integral, inseparable part of the financial report. In fact, financial reports state this on the bottom of each page of the financial statements, usually somewhat as follows:

> The accompanying footnotes to the financial statements are an integral part of these statements.

The auditor's report (see the next chapter) covers the footnotes as well as the financial statements. In short, footnotes are necessary for *adequate disclosure* in financial reports.

Two Basic Types of Footnotes

Basically, there are two kinds of footnotes. First, the major *accounting policies* of the business have to be identified and briefly explained. Its cost of goods sold expense method has to be identified (see Chapter 21 for discussion of these methods). And its depreciation method has to be identified (see Chapter 22). In short, if more than one generally accepted accounting method is allowed, the company's choice of method has to be disclosed. (Chapter 20 discusses the manager's responsibility for these key accounting choices.)

In addition to the key accounting choices of the business, other accounting premises and methods used to prepare the financial statements may be disclosed in footnotes. For example, many larger businesses consist of a family of corporations under the control of one parent corporation. Separate corporations are consolidated into one set of financial statements. However, affiliated companies in which the company has an equity interest but *not a controlling* interest are *not* consolidated.

The second type of footnotes provide *additional disclosure* that cannot be placed in the main body of the financial statements. For example, the maturity dates, interest rates, collateral or other security provisions, and other details of the long-term debt of a business are presented in a footnote; annual rentals required under operating leases are given; details regarding any stock option or employee stock ownership plans are spelled out; and the status of major lawsuits and other legal actions against the company are discussed.

Details about its employees' retirement and pension plans are also disclosed. Pension plan disclosure, in fact, is very complex but very important. The list of possible footnotes is a long one. In summary, many Balance Sheet accounts need additional footnote disclosure.

The Manager's Decision Regarding Footnotes

Managers have to rely on the experts—their chief accounting officer or the CPA auditor—to go through the checklist of footnotes that may be required. Once each required footnote has been identified, the manager should realize that there is still an important decision to make regarding each footnote. There is still a fair amount of management discretion or judgment required regarding just how frank to be, and how much detail to reveal in the footnote.

Clearly the manager should not divulge information that would cause a loss of or decline in any competitive advantage the business now enjoys. Managers don't have to help their competitors—the idea is to help the debtholders and stockholders of the business, to report to them information they are entitled to. But just how much information do the debtholders and stockholders need, or are they legally entitled to? This question is very difficult to answer. Beyond certain minimum basics and details, the extent of "required" or "fair" disclosure in footnotes is *not* at all clear.

Too little disclosure, such as withholding information about a major lawsuit against the business, for instance, would be misleading and the top managers are legally liable for this lack of disclosure. Beyond this "legal minimum," which will be insisted on by the CPA auditors, rules and guidelines are vague and murky. The manager has a fairly broad freedom of choice in how far to go and how frank to be.

Incomprehensible Footnotes:
A Serious Problem to Creditors and Investors

One last point concerns the readability of footnotes. As an author I may be overly sensitive to this, but I think not. Footnote writing sometimes is so poor that you have to suspect that the writing is deliberately obscure. The rules require footnotes, but the rules do not require that the footnotes be clear and concise so the average financial report reader can understand them.

Frequently the sentence structure of footnotes seems intentionally legalistic and awkward. Terminology is very technical. Poor writing seems more prevalent in footnotes on sensitive matters, such as lawsuits lost or still in progress, or ventures the business has abandoned with heavy losses. A lack of candor in many footnotes is obvious.

Creditors and stockholders cannot expect managers to expose all the dirty wash of the business in footnotes, or to confess all their bad decisions. But more clarity and honesty certainly would help and would not damage the business.

The stockholders can ask questions at their annual meetings with management and the board of directors. However, managers can be just as evasive in their answers as in the footnotes.

In short, creditors and investors frequently are stymied by poorly written footnotes. You really have only one choice, and that's to plow slowly through the troublesome footnotes, more than once if necessary. Usually you can tell if the footnote is important enough to deserve this extra effort.

19

THE COST OF CREDIBILITY—
AUDITS BY CPAs

Why Audits?

Suppose you have invested a lot of money in a business but are not involved in managing the company. You're an "absentee owner." As one of the owners you receive the company's financial reports. The previous chapters have explained how to read and understand the reports. But, how do you know that the financial reports are correct? Can you rely on the reports?

Or, suppose you are a bank loan officer and a business presents its financial report as part of the loan application package. Are the financial statements correct? How do you know?

Or, consider a corporation whose stock shares are traded on the New York Stock Exchange. The market value of the shares depends on the earnings record and other information presented in its financial reports. How do the stockholders know that the corporation's financial reports are correct?

The answer to this basic question is to have financial reports audited by independent *certified public accountants*. Based on the audit the CPA expresses an opinion on the financial report—an opinion that the business has followed generally acceptable accounting and disclosure standards in preparing its financial report. This opinion provides assurance that the financial report can be relied on by creditors and investors. In short, audits increase the credibility of financial reports.

Who's a certified public accountant? What is an audit of a company's financial statements? Are audits by CPAs required? Even if not required, should a business have its financial statements audited by an independent CPA? What are the limits of audits by CPAs? Do CPAs look for fraud? Will they catch all errors? Should a business use an outside CPA to help prepare its financial statements but *not* have its statements audited? What other services do CPAs offer to business?

These are the main questions addressed in this chapter.

Certified versus
Noncertified Public Accountants

A person needs to do three things to become a *certified* public accountant (CPA). He or she must earn a college degree with a fairly heavy major (emphasis) in accounting courses. Then the person must pass the national uniform CPA exam. Third, a person needs practical, on-the-job experience working for a CPA firm (in most states).

After all three basic requirements are completed—education, passing the CPA exam, and experience—the person receives the license by his or her state of residence to practice as a CPA. No one else may hold himself or herself out as a CPA. Most states require continuing education requirements to be satisfied to renew the CPA license. The State Boards of Accountancy in all states maintain a directory of those licensed to practice as a CPA in that state.

Those who have not met all the requirements can offer accounting and income tax services to the public, although they seldom do audits. They are called public accountants, or registered accountants. The use of this title and the regulation of non-CPAs vary from state to state. The main reason public accountants are not CPAs is that they have not passed the CPA exam, which is very rigorous and requires thorough preparation to pass.

Are Audits by CPAs Required?

Publicly owned corporations whose debt and/or stock securities are traded on a stock exchange or over-the-counter are required by federal securities laws to have their annual financial reports audited by an independent CPA firm. These include about 10,000 corporations in the United States today.

Beyond this group it is more difficult to generalize about which businesses are legally required to have their financial reports audited by CPAs, either annually or on certain occasions. There may be a legal need for an audit when raising capital through issuing debt or equity securities, even if the securities do not come under federal law. Lawyers should be consulted regarding state corporation and securities laws. Also, as a condition of borrowing money or issuing stock, a business can agree to have its annual financial reports audited.

But there are thousands and thousands of businesses that are not legally required to have their financial statements audited by CPAs. Neither federal nor state laws require the audits, and the businesses have not bound themselves by contract to have audits.

Even if Not Required, Should a Business Have Its Financial Report Audited by an Independent CPA?

Basically, audits by independent CPAs add *credibility* to the financial statements of a business. Audited financial statements have a higher credibility index than unaudited ones.

Two factors may cause the unaudited financial statements of a business to be wrong and seriously misleading:

1. *Honest mistakes* resulting from an inadequate accounting system or an inadequate understanding of accounting principles and financial reporting standards.

2. *Deliberate dishonesty* by a business manager who distorts the amounts reported in the financial statements or withholds important information.

Audits guard against both of these causes of misleading financial statements. Auditors are expert accounting system "detectives," and they thoroughly understand accounting principles and reporting standards. And, being independent of the business, the CPA auditor will not tolerate management dishonesty in the financial statements.

Be warned that the cost of an audit is high. The business manager cannot really bargain over how much auditing will be done. An audit is an audit. The CPA is bound by generally accepted auditing standards (GAAS), which are the authoritative rules in doing audits. There is no such thing as a "bargain basement" audit, or a "quick and dirty, once over lightly" audit. Violations of GAAS can result in legal suits against the CPA or may damage the CPA's professional reputation.

An audit requires a lot of work before the auditor can express an opinion on the financial statements (including footnotes). This results in the relatively high cost of an audit. The manager has to ask whether the gain in credibility is worth the cost of an audit.

A bank may insist on regular audits as a condition of making loans to a business. Or, those stockholders not directly involved in the day-to-day management of the business may insist on annual audits to protect their investment in the business. In these cases the audit is a cost of using "outside" capital. But in many situations the outside sources of capital do not insist on audits. In these cases should a business have an audit?

Perhaps one or more of its employees are stealing money or other assets, accepting kickbacks, or manipulating sales prices for relatives or friends. The record of employee theft and dishonesty is not a good one, unfortunately. An audit may uncover employee theft and dishonesty, or deter potential theft and dishonesty. But this is *not* the main purpose of an audit of financial reports.

A business should not have an audit if, in fact, it wants a security check. The business should ask the CPA to come in and closely study and evaluate its internal controls to deter and detect employee theft and dishonesty. This sort of investigation may be very useful, but it is *not* an audit of the financial report, which is for a different purpose.

What Are Audits? What's a Clean Opinion?

First, let's be very clear on one point. We're talking about audits of financial reports by CPAs. There are many other types of audits, such as audits by the Internal Revenue Service of taxpayer returns, audits of federally supported programs by the General Accounting Office, in-house audits by the internal auditors of an organization, and so on. The following discussion concerns audits of financial reports by CPAs for the purpose of the CPA expressing an opinion on the report.

Financial report users are not too concerned about how an audit is done, nor should they be. The bottom line to them is the opinion of the CPA. They should read the opinion carefully, although there is some evidence that most don't. Evidently, many users simply assume that having the financial report audited is, itself, an adequate check, or safeguard. They may assume that the CPA would not be associated with any financial report that is misleading or incorrect.

You've heard of "guilt by association" haven't you? Well, you could say that in the case of audits by CPAs there's a kind of reverse approach. Many, perhaps most, users of financial reports assume "innocence by association"—if the CPA gives an opinion and thereby is associated with the financial report, then the report must be OK, or at least not seriously misleading. Doesn't the CPA's opinion constitute a "stamp of approval"? Not necessarily!

The CPA auditing profession has gone to great lengths to define the limits of the audit opinion and to differentiate between several types of audit opinions.

The best audit opinion is called an *unqualified* opinion, or more popularly a "clean" opinion. Basically, this opinion states that the CPA has no material disagreements with the financial report. In other words, the CPA attests that the financial report has been prepared according to generally accepted accounting and disclosure principles. (This still leaves management a wide range of choices, as the next chapter explains.)

In a clean opinion the CPA auditor says "I don't disagree with the financial report." The CPA might have prepared the report differently; in fact, the CPA might prefer that different accounting methods had been used. All the CPA says in a clean opinion is that the accounting and disclosure presented in the financial report is acceptable.

Starting with 1988 financial reports the auditor's standard unqualified, or "clean" opinion report reads as follows:

Independent Auditor's Report

We have audited the accompanying balance sheets of X Company as of December 31, 19X2 and 19X1, and the related statements of income, retained earnings, and cash flows for the years then ended. These financial statements are the responsibility of the Company's management. Our responsibility is to express an opinion on these financial statements based on our audits.

We conducted our audits in accordance with generally accepted auditing standards. Those standards require that we plan and perform the audit to obtain reasonable assurance about whether the financial statements are free of material misstatement. An audit includes examining, on a test basis, evidence supporting the amounts and disclosures in the financial statements. An audit also includes assessing the accounting principles used and significant estimates made by management, as well as evaluating the overall financial statement presentation. We believe that our audits provide a reasonable basis for our opinion.

In our opinion, the financial statements referred to above present fairly, in all material respects, the financial position of X Company as of December 31, 19X2 and 19X1, and results of its operations and its cash flows for the years then ended in conformity with generally accepted accounting principles.

This new wording was adopted by the national professional association of CPAs, the American Institute of Certified Public Accountants (AICPA), to close the "expectations gap" by users of financial reports. The AICPA was of the opinion that investors and creditors did not adequately understand the primary role of management in preparing the financial report, so this point is mentioned in the first paragraph. Also, the AICPA thought that it should be made clear that audits provide reasonable but not absolute assurance that the financial statements are free of material accounting errors and provide all significant disclosures. Last, it was thought that the users of financial statements should be told briefly what an audit involves.

Whether the new wording will in fact close the expectations gap is open to question. The new version runs 200 words of fairly technical jargon, which asks a lot of the reader. In my opinion, creditors and investors will still have the same basic expectation—that they can rely on audited financial statements.

Financial statements that have been "blessed" with a clean opinion by the CPA auditor may later turn out to have been misleading, causing losses to creditors and investors. The auditor will probably be sued in these situations.

Overall, audits have an excellent track record—very few fraudulent or materially misleading financial reports get by the CPA auditor with a clean opinion. But a few do; audits are not perfect. The cost of an audit that would increase the probability of catching all material errors and all fraudulent intrigues to 100% would be prohibitive. There are occasional audit failures. The cost of eliminating all audit failures is too high a price to pay. In the grand scheme of things a few audit failures are tolerated to control the overall cost of audits.

What Are the Limits of Audits? Do CPAs Look for Fraud? Will They Catch All Errors?

To get to the point directly, auditors do *not* catch everything. If top-level managers cleverly conceal their own dishonesty or illegal acts and lie to the auditors as part of the cover-up, it's unlikely the auditors will discover this sort of high-level fraud. The auditors may find other evidence of such fraud, but the chances are not good. There are many cases where management fraud has gone on several years before coming to light, and then usually not by audit discovery. In short, audits (of financial reports) cannot be relied on to uncover all high-level management dishonesty and illegal acts.

What about unintentional errors that may creep into the accounting recordkeeping process during the year? If there is a repetitive pattern of these errors, the auditors are likely to catch these errors. On the other hand, if the errors are few and random in occurrence, the auditor may not catch the errors unless the errors result in a material overstatement or understatement of the year-end balance in an asset or liability.

The auditor takes samples from each of the populations of different transactions that took place during the year. Each sample is not big, but it is selected very carefully and the items in the sample are examined very closely. So if the errors follow a pattern of repetition, there usually will be one or more errors in the sample. But the occasional, nonrepetitive type of error may not be included in the sample. However, the auditor does a lot of work to verify the ending balances of the assets, liabilities, and owners' equities. If an error has carried forward and affects the ending balance, there is a high chance that the auditor will catch it.

Last, what about employee theft and dishonesty? CPA auditors are very concerned about this. The auditor carefully studies and evaluates the company's internal accounting controls that are designed to deter and detect errors as well as intentional irregularities by employees. If controls are weak, more audit procedures are directed to the weak areas. Serious weaknesses are called to management's attention.

Nevertheless, collusion among two or more employees who work together in a conspiracy to cheat the business is difficult for the auditor to discover. Also, unrecorded transactions, such as skimming off the top of sales revenue, are difficult to discover. To the extent possible, a business is wise to employ other precautions such as rotation of duties among employees and, while employees take their vacations, assigning a replacement to do the work of the employee on vacation. A business should not rely on the audit alone. In fact, CPAs will (or should) tell managers to institute such controls.

Additional Language in Unqualified Opinions and Qualified Opinions

In some situations the CPA auditor must extend the unqualified (clean) opinion with additional explanatory comments. The standard clean opinion consists of three rather long paragraphs (see page 108). Nevertheless, a fourth paragraph is necessary: (a) if there are major uncertainties that cannot be estimated in any reasonable manner and, thus, are not yet accounted for in the financial statements; (b) the company has changed its accounting principles or methods between this and previous years; and (c) there is substantial doubt about the entity's ability to continue as a going concern. All three of these situations are very important for creditors and investors to be aware of, so the AICPA has decided that they should be mentioned in the auditor's report.

A *qualified* audit opinion is issued when the CPA takes exception to an accounting method used by the company or when the CPA finds fault with the disclosure in the financial report. The CPA is satisfied that the financial report taken as a whole is not misleading but nevertheless takes exception with one or more items in the statement because the company has departed from the established rules, i.e., generally accepted accounting principles. The Securities and Exchange Commission (SEC) generally will not accept qualified audit reports, because the company could change its accounting or disclosure to avoid the qualified opinion. For nonpublic companies, however, you'll see qualified opinions.

How serious a matter is a qualified opinion? Basically, it's a "fly in the ointment" effect. The auditor is pointing out a flaw in the financial report, but not a fatal flaw. It's a yellow flag, but not a red flag. The auditor must be satisfied that the overall fairness of the financial report is satisfactory, even though there are one or more departures from established accounting and disclosure standards. If the auditor is of the opinion that the exceptions are so serious as to make the financial report misleading, the CPA must go much further and give an *adverse* opinion. You hardly ever see an adverse opinion. No company wants to issue misleading financial reports and have the auditor say so.

Using a CPA to Review or Prepare Financial Statements Instead of Auditing Them

An audit may be too costly; the cost of the audit could be more than the interest on the loan to a smaller business. Bankers and other sources of loans to business understand this. Often lenders do not insist on an audit. Yet they prefer that a CPA at least "look over" the financial reports of companies they loan money to.

A CPA can perform certain limited procedures called a *review*. A review is *far less* than a full-scale audit. But a review does provide the CPA with a basis of information about the financial report. Based on the review, the CPA can state that he or she is not aware of any modifications (changes) that are needed to make the financial statements conform with generally accepted accounting principles. This is said in the final paragraph of the CPA's report. However, the CPA (reviewer) also warns the reader earlier in the report that a review is substantially less than an audit and that, accordingly, no opinion is being expressed on the financial report.

In short, based on a review the CPA does not give an affirmative opinion report; instead, the auditor gives a negative assurance ("no modifications are needed . . ."). This negative assurance may be enough to satisfy the lender.

An audit or a review by a CPA is made of the financial statements prepared by the business itself. Many smaller companies, on the other hand, need the help of a CPA to prepare their financial statements in the first place. These companies don't have a professionally qualified accountant on their payroll. They use a CPA as a "part-time Controller" (chief accountant) to pull together their financial statements.

In this situation the CPA is said to *compile* the financial statements. No audit and no review is done; so, the CPA must disclaim any opinion on the financial report, and no negative assurance may be given either.

Other Services of CPAs

It's not too much of an exaggeration to say that the last decade has seen more changes in how CPA firms carry on their practice than the previous century. CPA firms have become much more aggressive in promoting their services and have become much more competitive with one another, compared with the traditional, more conservative way of doing things.

Originally the audit function was the main activity of CPA firms. Then, there was the tremendous explosion of the federal income tax law starting with World War II and continuing until today. The income tax services of CPA firms expanded to keep pace. CPAs stand ready to provide almost any tax service you might want. CPAs are rightly viewed as tax experts. They offer their services to all kinds of taxpayers—individuals, estates, trusts, partnerships, and corporations. Given the complexity of income tax laws it's no wonder that CPAs are needed to provide advice and counsel, as well as for the actual preparation and filing of tax returns.

Recently CPA firms have extended their management consulting services beyond the traditional accounting-based areas, into many areas far removed from financial statements and accounting systems. Today CPA firms offer consulting services in the design and operation of manufacturing systems, in the broad area of personal financial planning, in the area of pensions and other employee compensation plans, in the area of computer systems, and so on. Many CPA firms have departments that specialize in consulting with smaller, emerging businesses. The future will probably see more changes in the consulting area than in audit and tax services. In short, the modern CPA firm is in three lines of business—audit, tax, and consulting.

20

MANIPULATING THE
NUMBERS
(OR, COOKING THE BOOKS)

The Name of the Game

Financial reports are prepared in conformity with certain established standards called *Generally Accepted Accounting Principles* (GAAP). Rarely, if ever, would you come across a financial report of a business that states GAAP have not been followed. Audits of financial reports by CPAs are precisely for the purpose of making sure that the company has complied with GAAP in preparing its financial report (see Chapter 19).

Basically, a business has to *play fair* in reporting its profit-making operations (Income Statement), its financial condition (Balance Sheet), and its cash flows (Cash Flow Statement)—as well as providing additional disclosure in footnotes. In other words, the established standards (GAAP) should be followed in measuring sales revenue and expenses to determine profit (net income) and to determine asset, liability, and owners' equity values—the "numbers."

You may assume that once the facts of a company's transactions and operations have been determined there emerges one and only one set of accounting numbers. However, you should know that the same facts do *not* lead to the same numbers. Financial accounting would seem to be like measuring a person's weight, wouldn't it? But in fact, financial accounting also involves choosing the scale—one that weighs light or one that weighs heavy, or possibly one that weighs in between. In short, for many financial statement numbers there's not just one rule, but two rules or even three rules. The game can be played fairly by any one of the rules. Choices must be made from among *alternative* equally accepted accounting methods.

The conditions of each case do *not* dictate the method that has to be used. For example, in periods of rising costs, either a conservative "keep the profits down" Cost of Goods Sold Expense method may be used, or a more generous method may be used. And in periods of stable costs, either method may be selected. For another example, regardless of whether long-lived asset replacement costs are increasing or holding level, either a rapid (accelerated) or slower (straight-line) depreciation method may be used. The selection of the depreciation method does not depend on what's happening to replacement costs of the company's fixed assets.

Many deplore this "looseness" or "elasticity" of accounting methods. In theory, one accounting method would seem the preferred or best method in particular circumstances. In other words, specific conditions would seem to lead to one and only one accounting method. So if two different businesses were in the same set of circumstances, their accounting methods would be the same. But in fact, their accounting methods might be different.

The authoritative pronouncements on GAAP over the years have narrowed down the range of acceptable methods, to be sure. But within this range there are still choices to be made. For an illustration, see Exhibit I on the next page.

The chief executive has to make certain that the company's financial statements stay within the bounds of fairness, that is, that the accounting choices are those in the range of GAAP. If the accounting methods are outside these limits, the financial statements will be false and misleading, and the manager will be liable for damages suffered by those debtholders and stockholders who relied on the statements. If for no other reason than this, the manager should pay close attention to the choice of accounting methods used to prepare the company's financial statement numbers.

Once an accounting method is decided upon, the business must, for all practical purposes, stick with the method consistently year to year. So, if a business chooses a conservative set of accounting methods, its financial statements will continue to be conservative for many years.

Last, it should be mentioned that the real, or ultimate driving force behind the accounting numbers is the profit-making ability of management—making sales and controlling expenses. The choice of accounting methods makes a difference, to be sure, but only in a marginal sense, not in a fundamental sense.

EXHIBIT I—THE RANGE OF ACCOUNTING METHODS

Unacceptable Methods That Would Be too Conservative	*Range of Acceptable Accounting Methods (choice of methods within this range are in conformity with generally accepted accounting principles)*		*Unacceptable Methods That Would Be too Liberal*
- - - - - - - - - - - -	← - →		- - - - - - - - - - -
	← - - - - - - - - INCOME STATEMENT - - - - - - - - →		
—Arbitrarily charging off to expense now the cost of inventory that will not be sold until later	—Annual profit is measured as low as possible; sales revenue is recorded at lowest possible amounts, and expenses are recorded at highest possible amounts.	—Annual profit is measured as high as possible; sales revenue is recorded at highest possible amounts, and expenses are recorded at lowest possible amounts.	—Not writing off the cost of unsalable inventory
—Charging to expense now the cost of a major long-lived asset that will be used for several more years			—Depreciation of a long-lived asset over a much longer period than it will be useful to the business
	← - - - - - - - - - - BALANCE SHEET - - - - - - - - - - →		
—Recording expenses for vague and nonspecific contingency losses that probably will not happen	—Assets are recorded as low as possible because expenses are charged out at highest amounts or at earliest time, and thus the assets involved contain the smallest cost residuals.	—Assets are recorded as high as possible because expenses are charged out at lowest amounts or at latest time and thus the assets involved contain the largest cost residuals.	—Failure to recognize the impending loss from lawsuits or other assessments the business will have to pay.
—Delaying the recording of sales that have been made in the ordinary course of business	—Certain liabilities are recorded at highest amounts because the expenses involving these liabilities are recorded at the largest amounts possible.	—Certain liabilities are recorded at lowest amounts because the expenses involving the liabilities are recorded at the lowest amounts possible.	—Recording sales before the sales are final, or failure to recognize the likelihood of large returns of products or large bad debts.

Note: Cash flows are not affected by the choice of accounting methods, except that methods used for income tax will affect the income tax payments during the year.

Managers Should Manipulate the Numbers

Business managers may try to avoid getting involved in choosing accounting methods. But this is a mistake. First, there is the risk that the financial statements may not be prepared according to GAAP in one or more respects. Using CPAs to audit the financial statements minimizes the risk of releasing misleading statements. However, even financial statements that have been audited by very respectable CPA firms have been found deficient; managers and CPAs have been found guilty in court trials, and they have had to pay large damages to debtholders and stockholders. Managers certainly have to keep aware of the consequences of reporting misleading financial statements. But there is a more important reason for managers getting involved in making accounting choices.

The business manager should decide which accounting methods best fit the general policies and philosophy of the business. In other words, the manager has to decide which "look" of the financial statements is in the best interests of the company. Putting it more crudely, the manager can and should manipulate the profit numbers, and the asset and liability numbers that are reported in the financial statements.

The point is this: the numbers have to be manipulated— if not by the managers, then by their accountants. By staying out of the decision making, the manager allows the accountant to do the manipulating. But the accountant may not be fully aware of all the policies of the company and the various pressures on the business. The manager may, given all the pressures and problems at the present time, need a rather "aggressive" set of financial statements, say to persuade the bank to make a loan or to convince a major customer of the financial ability of the company to carry through on a major deal or a long-term contract. But the accountant may choose conservative accounting methods instead.

The managers should select those accounting methods that best advance the interests of the business. The manager should ask whether the accounting methods of the business should be on the conservative end, in the middle, or on the liberal end of the range of generally accepted methods. These are not easy decisions. But the decisions are too important to leave to the accountant alone. And in the process of getting involved, the manager will certainly develop a much better understanding of financial statements, which helps in analyzing profit performance and financial position and in "talking" the financial statements when borrowing money or when raising equity capital.

Are Investors Fooled by Accounting Methods?

Like it or not, we live in a world of alternative accounting methods. Choices have to be made. Thus, financial statements are flexible. The financial statements for a business can be presented in a "small, medium, or large size," depending on which specific accounting methods managers select to account for profit. GAAP permit this elasticity in the numbers reported in financial statements.

Management must disclose in footnotes which accounting methods have been selected to prepare their financial statements (see Chapter 18). So, investors can determine whether the business is being conservative or not so conservative in reporting its net income and financial condition. There is a fair amount of evidence, based on research studies, that investors make allowances for different accounting methods when comparing different companies. Also, studies show that when a company changes its accounting methods there is not a "knee jerk" reaction to the new numbers reported by the company. Market value tends to remain the same, other things being the same. In short, investors are not fooled by the arbitrary selection or change of accounting methods by companies.

The overall conservatism of the financial statements of a business depends on two accounting methods in particular—the method to measure Cost of Goods Sold Expense and the depreciation method. To be sure, other important accounting methods may have a large impact on profit accounting. But the Cost of Goods Sold Expense method and the depreciation method set the tone for most businesses. The next two chapters examine these two important, benchmark accounting methods.

21

THE COST OF GOODS SOLD
CONUNDRUM

The Importance of This Accounting Decision: Introducing the Example

The cost of products sold to customers usually is a company's largest single expense, commonly being 60–70% of sales revenue. Gross margin and all the profit lines below gross margin are very sensitive to how the Cost of Goods (products) Sold Expense is measured. Clearly, managers have a high stake in how much profit is earned, so managers should understand how the biggest deduction against sales revenue is measured. As a matter of fact, the chief executive should make the accounting decision regarding which method shall be used by the business to measure its Cost of Goods Sold Expense.

Three basic methods are widely used to determine the Cost of Goods Sold Expense. All three methods have theoretical support, and all three methods are acceptable interpretations of the general accounting principle that cost of goods sold should be deducted against sales revenue in the same period to measure gross margin for the period.

A specific example is needed to demonstrate the accounting problem and to contrast the differences in profit and inventory values between the three methods. The starting point is *product cost*. For a manufacturer this is production cost; for a retailer this is purchase cost. A problem arises when product cost changes over time, when the next batch manufactured or the next batch purchased has a unit cost different from the one before. This is true for almost all businesses, of course!

Suppose a company sold 4,000 units of a product during the year. The company began the year with 1,000 units, which is the carryforward stock from the end of last year. Few companies would let their inventory level drop to zero. So, assume the company replaced products as they were sold during the year and ended the year with 1,000 units, the same quantity as its beginning inventory. To keep the example relatively easy to follow but fairly realistic at the same time, assume the company made four acquisitions of products during the year, each of 1,000 units. In short, the company replaced the units sold but did not increase or decrease its inventory level.

Exhibit J presents the facts of the example. Notice in particular that each successive acquisition cost $5,000 more than the one before. Now, before we proceed, I'd like to get your opinion on this accounting problem. How would you divide the total cost of the 5,000 units between the 4,000 units sold and the

EXHIBIT J—COST OF GOODS SOLD & INVENTORY EXAMPLE
Facts of Example and Questions

Batch	Quantity	Cost
Beginning Inventory	1,000 units	$100,000
First Acquisition	1,000	105,000
Second Acquisition	1,000	110,000
Third Acquisition	1,000	115,000
Fourth Acquisition	1,000	120,000
Totals	5,000 units	$550,000
Less: Goods Sold	4,000	???
Equals: Ending Inventory	1,000 units	???

1,000 units still on hand in inventory at year-end? (See Exhibit J again.)

I think you'd agree that the $550,000 total cost of the 5,000 units should be divided between the Cost of Goods Sold Expense for the 4,000 units sold during the year and the Inventory asset account at year-end for the 1,000 units not yet sold (but will be sold next year).

Suppose you are the chief executive of this company. How would you divide the cost? No fair sitting on the sidelines and letting the accountant decide how to do it. Too often managers simply go along with the method recommended by accountants without analyzing the situation for themselves. This is not a good idea. The choice is a management decision, which should be made like other management decisions—What are the alternatives? What are the consequences of each alternative? Which alternative is the best relative to the company's goals and other relevant criteria?

The Average Cost Method

My guess is that you would intuitively choose the *Average Cost Method*, as shown on this page. You would argue that ⅘ of the goods were sold, so ⅘ of the total cost should be charged to Cost of Goods Sold Expense, and ⅕ should be allocated to ending Inventory. Put another way, the average cost per unit is $110.00 ($550,000/5,000 units = $110.00). This average cost is multiplied times the number of units sold to get the $440,000 Cost of Goods Sold Expense. The logic is that we are determining the gross margin for the whole year, so it makes sense to pool all costs for the year and then let each unit share and share alike, whether the unit was sold or is still in inventory at year-end.

However, the Average Cost Method runs a distant third in popularity. Much more likely the company would select one of two other methods. These are explained next.

EXHIBIT J—COST OF GOODS SOLD & INVENTORY EXAMPLE
Average Cost Method

Batch	Quantity	Cost
Beginning Inventory	1,000 units	$100,000
First Acquisition	1,000	105,000
Second Acquisition	1,000	110,000
Third Acquisition	1,000	115,000
Fourth Acquisition	1,000	120,000
Totals	5,000 units	$550,000
Less: Goods Sold	4,000	440,000
Equals: Ending Inventory	1,000 units	$110,000

The Last-In, First-Out (LIFO) Method

The last-in, first-out, or LIFO method, selects the four batches that were purchased during the year and charges this $450,000 total cost to expense (see Exhibit J). The last-in, or most recent purchases are the first charged out to expense. Purchase costs increased during the year, so LIFO maximizes the Cost of Goods Sold Expense. The beginning inventory batch, in this example the $100,000 cost of inventory at the start of the year, remains as the cost of the ending inventory at the close of the year. The actual products on hand at the end of the year are those bought most recently. Nevertheless, LIFO allows the cost of ending inventory to be the residual batch left over after selecting the more recent batches to charge to expense for the year. Thus the LIFO method allocates to ending inventory the "old" $100,000 cost.

The primary theory of the LIFO method is that products sold have to be replaced to continue in business, and that the most recent (i.e., the last-in) costs are the closest to the costs of replacing the products sold. When there is cost inflation (as in this example), LIFO maximizes the Cost of Goods Sold Expense and thus minimizes the profit reported in the Income Statement. To do this, however, inventory is reported at the lowest cost in the Balance Sheet.

EXHIBIT J—COST OF GOODS SOLD & INVENTORY EXAMPLE
Last-In, First-Out (LIFO) Method

Batch	Quantity	Cost
Beginning Inventory	1,000 units	$100,000
First Acquisition	1,000	105,000
Second Acquisition	1,000	110,000
Third Acquisition	1,000	115,000
Fourth Acquisition	1,000	120,000
Totals	5,000 units	$550,000
Less: Goods Sold	4,000	450,000
Equals: Ending Inventory	1,000 units	$100,000

The First-In, First-Out (FIFO) Method

The reverse of the LIFO method is the first-in, first-out, or FIFO method. The FIFO method selects the beginning inventory batch and the first, second, and third acquisitions during the year, and charges this $430,000 total cost to expense (see Exhibit J). The first batches in are the first batches to be charged out to expense. The $120,000 cost batch, being the last purchase during the year, becomes the cost of the ending inventory.

The primary theory of FIFO is that the actual flow of products usually is a first-in, first-out sequence. When there is cost inflation during the year (as in this example), FIFO minimizes the cost of goods sold expense and thus maximizes the profit reported in the Income Statement. And inventory is reported at the highest cost in the Balance Sheet.

EXHIBIT J—COST OF GOODS SOLD & INVENTORY EXAMPLE
First-In, First-Out (FIFO) Method

Batch	Quantity	Cost
Beginning Inventory	1,000	100,000
First Acquisition	1,000	105,000
Second Acquisition	1,000	110,000
Third Acquisition	1,000	115,000
Fourth Acquisition	1,000	120,000
Totals	5,000 units	$550,000
Less: Goods Sold	4,000	430,000
Equals: Ending Inventory	1,000 units	$120,000

What Difference Does It Make?

In this example purchase costs increased 20% during the year, which is not unrealistic given the inflationary environment of business. LIFO results in $20,000 less reported gross margin compared with the FIFO method. In other words, LIFO gives a Cost of Goods Sold Expense that is $20,000 more than FIFO. Assume that total sales revenue from the 4,000 units sold during the year was $645,000 based on gross margin equal to ⅓ of sales revenue, which is the experience of the company in this example. (The sales revenue amount is developed in more detail later in this chapter.) The $20,000 difference between LIFO and FIFO is about 3% of sales revenue.

And what about inventory? Ending inventory is reported at $100,000 cost by LIFO, compared to $120,000 cost by FIFO (see Exhibit J). LIFO causes the asset to be reported at ⅙ less cost than FIFO in the Balance sheet. This penalizes the current ratio, a key solvency ratio discussed in Chapter 23. The company's total current assets will look smaller compared with its total current liabilities.

In brief summary: during periods of rising costs, LIFO results in the lowest reported profit and the lowest reported inventory cost. Why, therefore, do companies use LIFO? One possible reason is conservatism. They want to err on the downside and not be accused of overstating profits or assets. Another possible reason for LIFO is to minimize profits that are subject to profit-sharing plans for employees or second-level managers, or bonus plans based on profits. Keeping reported profits low keeps the profit shares or bonuses low. Another reason might be to "hide" profits during periods of labor problems or union contract bargaining. Also, a company may need to make the argument that it needs to earn more profit and thus has to raise its sales prices.

Or, the main reason may be to minimize *taxable income*. LIFO is allowed for income tax purposes. LIFO reduces taxable income by $20,000 compared with FIFO, so the income tax bill for the year would be less.

Cash flow is important. A business may be in a very tight cash situation and need to hang on to every dollar it can as long as possible. Even if not strapped for cash, the business probably can put the tax savings to work and earn a return on its investment. Last, if inflation continues the business might as well delay paying its income taxes as long as possible and pay off in the cheaper dollars of the future.

LIFO Liquidation Gains:
A Special Feature of LIFO

Once a business selects LIFO, it must remain consistent with it over the entire life cycle of the product. LIFO is a long-term commitment. (This is true for all accounting methods in most cases, as mentioned before.)

Furthermore, the business manager should think ahead about what happens in the last year of the product's life cycle. In the last year there is a *LIFO liquidation profit* that causes a rather large "blip," or one-time gain caused by selling out of the inventory. Refer again to Exhibit J on page 125. Now assume we are at a time 5 years later, and this product was phased out during this year. To simplify, assume that the company has kept its inventory at the same 1,000 units level.

During the last year, assume that the average cost of each purchase is $220,000, due to inflation every year since the year used in the example. Normally the company would make four purchases during the year and the total cost of these four purchases is charged to Cost of Goods Sold Expense by the LIFO method. *But*, in the last year the company makes only three purchases and liquidates all its inventory of 1,000 units to provide the rest of its sales. This "old batch" causes the problem.

The cost of the old batch that is charged to Cost of Goods Sold Expense is $100,000, not the current prevailing purchase cost of $220,000. So there is a one-time nonrecurring gain of $120,000 in gross margin! And, taxable income is also $120,000 higher as a result of the inventory liquidation.

All a business does by using LIFO is delay the reporting of a certain amount of profit, both in its annual Income Statements and its annual tax returns. Eventually, when the business reaches the end of the product's life cycle and liquidates its inventory, the profit that would have been recorded along the way by the FIFO method "catches up" with the business and has to be recorded.

Managers certainly should be aware of the eventual LIFO liquidation gain at the end of a product's life cycle. To go a step further on this point; the manager does not have to wait until the end of the life cycle. Instead, the manager could "force" this effect by deliberately allowing LIFO based inventory to fall below normal levels. Toward the end of the year the manager could hold off purchases, thus causing the ending inventory quantity to fall to abnormally low levels. Or, a severe business downturn may force the business to drastically reduce its inventory levels and thus to dip into its old LIFO layers.

In short, the business has some potential profit in reserve, or "on the shelf," in the form of inventory carried on the LIFO cost basis. There is nothing to prohibit management manipulation of reported profit by the partial liquidation of LIFO-based inventory. The manager can do this without any objection from the CPA auditing the financial statements, although such LIFO liquidation gains have to be reported in a footnote to the company's financial statements (if material).

Should the LIFO or FIFO Choice Be Consistent with Sales Pricing Policy?

Assume that you're the manager who sets sales prices for the product in the example. Needless to say, many factors and pressures affect sales prices. But to simplify somewhat, assume that normally you base your sales price on the most recent purchase cost and you let all the units in this batch go out at this sales price until you exhaust the batch. When you start selling from the next batch, you change your sales price based on the new cost of the next batch. As mentioned earlier, your sales price is based on a 50% markup on cost, which means that gross margin is $\frac{1}{3}$ of sales revenue. For example, if the purchase cost is $2.00, a $1.00 markup is added to get the $3.00 sales price.

Given these assumptions regarding sales pricing, your total sales revenue for the year is determined as follows (see Exhibit J for purchase costs):

Batch	Cost		50% Markup		Sales Revenue
Beginning Inventory	$100,000	+	$50,000	=	$150,000
First Acquisition	105,000	+	52,500	=	157,500
Second Acquisition	110,000	+	55,000	=	165,000
Third Acquisition	115,000	+	57,500	=	172,500
Total Sales Revenue for the Year					$645,000

This schedule should make clear that you are following a first-in, first-out, or FIFO, sales price policy.

You should be very interested in the results that would be reported in your annual Income Statement by the LIFO and FIFO methods:

INCOME STATEMENT

	LIFO		FIFO	
	Amount	Percent	Amount	Percent
Sales Revenue	$645,000	100.0	$645,000	100.0
Cost of Goods Sold	450,000	69.8	430,000	66.7
Gross Margin	$195,000	30.2	$215,000	33.3

FIFO gives results consistent with your sales price policy: the Cost of Goods Sold Expense is exactly $\frac{2}{3}$ (66.7%) of sales revenue, and gross margin is exactly $\frac{1}{3}$ (33.3%) of sales revenue.

LIFO, on the other hand, reports that you are falling short of your gross margin goal. Managers, of course, rely on Income Statements for feedback on profit performance. The LIFO method suggests that you should raise prices because your gross margin is only 30.2% of sales revenue. The LIFO method may be used to determine Cost of Goods Sold Expense. But this does not mean that the company is able to set its sales prices on the LIFO basis.

LIFO sales prices would be based on the *next* acquisition cost, i.e., the costs of replacing the units sold. In this example, the LIFO sales prices would be based on the four acquisitions shown in Exhibit J ($105,000, $110,000, $115,000, and $120,000). This would require total sales revenue of $675,000, instead of $645,000, or $30,000 more sales revenue.

But could the higher prices have been charged to customers? Normally competitive pressures keep sales prices down or delay the increase of sales prices. In short, a company's sales price policy may be "forced" by competitive pressures to stay on a FIFO basis. If costs of goods sold expense is on a LIFO basis, reported gross margin will be somewhat misleading. Managers definitely should keep this in mind when analyzing the gross margin performance numbers reported in their Income Statements. Likewise, creditors and investors should allow for this in evaluating a company's profit performance.

22

ACCELERATED OR STRAIGHT-LINE DEPRECIATION?

Long-Lived Assets as Capitalized Costs

When acquiring most long-lived assets, there are certain costs that could be put in asset accounts, but don't necessarily have to be. In pure theory these costs should be "capitalized," which means that the costs should be recorded in asset accounts and included in their total cost. As a practical matter, however, certain costs don't have to be capitalized.

For example, assume a business has just bought a new delivery truck. The purchase cost paid to the truck dealer has to be capitalized. Until the Tax Reform Act of 1986, however, the business had the option whether to capitalize the sales taxes paid on the truck. Now sales taxes must be included in the total cost of the truck.

The truck may be painted with the company's name, address, and logo. The business may put special racks or fittings in the truck. In theory, these additional costs should be capitalized and included in the asset account. But the costs are not directly a part of the purchase cost; the costs are, as a practical matter, detachable from the purchase cost.

Many long-lived asset acquisitions involve such additional detachable costs. New buildings certainly do. Beyond the basic contract price of a building the company usually has many additional moving-in and preparation costs. Likewise, in addition to the purchase cost of a new machine or a new piece of equipment, a business typically has installation costs.

Also, almost all businesses buy many tools such as hammers, power saws, drills, floor-cleaning machines, dollies, and so on. In theory the cost of these relatively low-cost tools should be capitalized if they will be used for more than one year.

For convenience the additional detachable costs associated with the acquisition of long-lived assets and the cost of small tools and like items will be called *gray area costs* in the following discussion.

Say a business has just purchased a new long-lived asset and has paid $50,000 cash for the asset. Shortly following the purchase the business incurs $5,000 additional gray area costs.

The $50,000 has to be capitalized, and accordingly is put in an asset account. If not, the CPA auditors would certainly object, and the IRS could accuse the business of tax evasion. In other words, charging off the $50,000 to expense immediately is clearly in violation of generally accepted accounting principles

EXHIBIT K—COMPARISON OF CAPITALIZING VERSUS NOT CAPITALIZING GRAY AREA COSTS

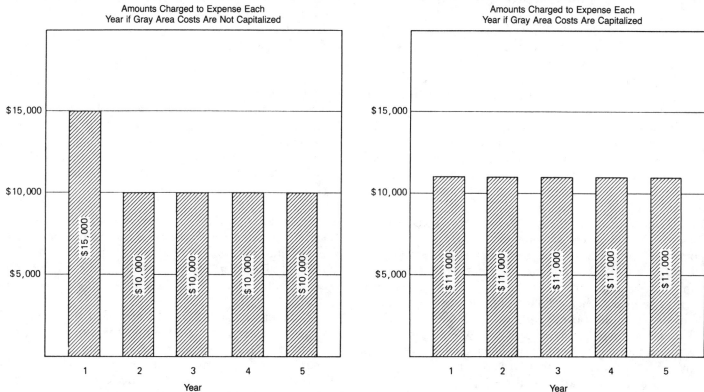

Amounts Charged to Expense Each
Year if Gray Area Costs Are Not Capitalized

Amounts Charged to Expense Each
Year if Gray Area Costs Are Capitalized

(GAAP) and income tax laws. The $50,000 has to be allocated over the future years of use expected from the asset. Chapter 10 explains the basic theory of depreciation accounting.

On the other hand, the business manager could decide to allow the $5,000 of gray area costs to fall into expense this period. Instead of capitalizing the additional $5,000, all this amount could be charged to expense this period. This penalizes this year's profits, but relieves the future years of this much additional depreciation expense.

Assume that the asset is depreciated over 5 years. Also assume that an equal amount of depreciation is charged to each year (just to simplify the example here). The impact on expenses for each year from the decision to capitalize versus not to capitalize the gray area costs is shown in Exhibit K on page 135.

Not to capitalize the gray area costs is very conservative. The first year's expenses absorb an extra $5,000, and the asset is reported at a lower cost value in the Balance Sheet. On the other hand, it must be remembered that in making this choice the company escapes a certain amount of depreciation expense in each future year. There is a "robbing Peter to pay Paul" effect. In the example above, year 1 is "robbed" by absorbing $4,000 additional expense, but years 2, 3, 4, and 5 are "paid" $1,000 additional profit. On the other hand, if the gray area costs are capitalized, each year is treated equally.

The main reason for not capitalizing gray area costs is to minimize taxable income in the first year (the year of acquiring long-lived assets). In the first year the amount paid out for taxes is lowered, and the company has the use of the tax saving until it has to be paid back in the future years. (Don't forget that taxable income in each of the future years is higher.) The cash flow advantage in the first year is very persuasive. This "free loan" from the government, plus the more conservative look of their financial statements, cause many managers not to capitalize gray area costs.

Last, the policy of not capitalizing gray area costs and charging them entirely to expense in the first year provides business managers another way to manipulate reported profit. The timing of many of these expenditures is somewhat discretionary. Small tools can be replaced at the end of this year, or replacement can be delayed to the start of next year. Thus the expense can be held off until next year. Also, the acquisition of several assets can be delayed and "slipped over" to the following year. So the associated gray area costs would not be recorded as expense until next year. In reverse, the purchase of small tools and fixed assets can be speeded up, and thus the gray area costs would be recorded as expense this year instead of next year.

On the other hand, it can be argued that without any deliberate management manipulation the amount of gray area costs tends to be more or less the same year to year. So, there is a more or less "washout" effect every year, and the net difference would be negligible. Indeed, for a mature business this may not be far off the mark.

Deciding on Useful Life Estimates and Depreciation Methods

A building may stand 60–100 years. Yet the Internal Revenue Code (IRC) allows a 31.5-year depreciation life for tax purposes. An office desk may last 20 years, yet the IRC allows a 7-year life for this type of asset. And so on.

In short, the federal income tax permits long-lived assets to be depreciated over life spans that are too short, compared with the actual typical useful lives of the assets. This is a deliberate policy of the federal government, to encourage investment and to allow business to recover capital invested in assets over a shorter time span than the actual useful lives of the assets.

It's fair to say that the federal tax laws regarding depreciation lives have removed any attempt to be realistic in estimating the useful life spans of long-lived assets. In brief, the shortest allowed lives are adopted by the large majority of businesses. These "short lives" are found in the Accelerated Cost Recovery System (ACRS) now a part of our federal income tax laws. In fact, there's hardly any point arguing for more realistic (longer) life estimates.*

---

* However, the 1986 Tax Reform Act does permit assets to be depreciated over longer life spans.

All financial statement users should keep in mind that long-lived assets are depreciated too fast—not in the actual wearing out or economic sense, mind you, but in the accounting/recordkeeping sense. The reported book values of these assets in Balance Sheets are very conservative for this reason. This, plus the rapid pace of inflation, means that after a few years the total book value of a company's long-lived assets is far below the total current replacement cost of the assets.

Basically, a business has two alternatives regarding depreciation of its long-lived assets:

1. Adopt the income-tax approach, which uses short lives for the assets, and which also allows a front-end "loading" through accelerated depreciation; or,

2. Adopt more realistic (longer) useful life estimates for the assets and spread the annual depreciation over the useful life of each asset according to the *straight-line* method. The straight-line method simply means allocating an equal amount of depreciation to each (full) year of use of the asset.

For example, assume a business buys a new machine. The income tax law allows this asset to be depreciated over 7 years.

Alternatively, the business may use a 12-year useful life estimate, which we'll assume to be realistic for this particular kind of machine. Exhibit L, on the next page, shows the difference in depreciation year by year, assuming the cost of the machine is $120,000.

Although accelerated depreciation has obvious income tax advantages, there are certain disadvantages. For one thing, the book (reported) values of long-lived assets are lower. (See Exhibit L again.) Some borrowing is done on the basis of these assets; mortgages or other liens may be given on the assets, or lenders may consider book values in their decisions. The lower book values of its long-lived assets may lower the debt capacity of a business by using accelerated depreciation.

One final point: managers and investors are very interested in the growth (or decline) of profit year to year. Ideally, a profit increase this year over last year should be due to "real" causes such as better profit margins on sales, operating efficiency improvements, higher volumes, and so forth. Spurious increases in reported profit are misleading to managers and investors. Profit trends are difficult to track reliably if there are accounting "drop-offs" in annual depreciation expense, such as shown in Exhibit L by the accelerated method. The straight-line method has the advantage of keeping the depreciation expense constant year to year (on the same assets).

EXHIBIT L—ACCELERATED VERSUS STRAIGHT-LINE DEPRECIATION EXAMPLE

(Machine Cost = $120,000; Accelerated = 7 Years; Straight-Line = 12 Years)

Year	Accelerated Depreciation	Straight-Line Depreciation	Cumulative Difference in Book Value of Asset at Year-End
1	$ 17,148	$ 5,000	$12,148
2	29,388	10,000	31,536
3	20,988	10,000	42,524
4	14,988	10,000	47,512
5	10,716	10,000	48,228
6	10,704	10,000	48,932
7	10,716	10,000	49,648
8	5,352	10,000	45,000
9		10,000	35,000
10		10,000	25,000
11		10,000	15,000
12		10,000	5,000
13		5,000	0
Totals	$120,000	$120,000	

Note: Accelerated method based on Double-Declining Balance method with half-year convention and switch to Straight-Line method when advantageous; Straight-Line method based on half-year convention.

23

**RATIOS FOR CREDITORS
AND INVESTORS**

When deciding whether to make or renew loans to businesses, bankers and other lenders direct their attention to particular financial statement ratios. Credit rating agencies, such as Dun & Bradstreet, compile financial statement ratios on thousands of businesses. The ratios provide a statistical profile of a business, for assessing its credit worthiness and the risk in extending credit to the business. If a company's ratios are weak, securing loans and trade credit becomes difficult.

Stock investors also focus on particular financial statement ratios. They are first concerned about whether the business will be able to pay its debts when they come due, as well as the overall liability situation of the business. Maintaining solvency (debt-paying ability) is essential for continuing operations, of course. Therefore, investors are interested in the same ratios as those looked at by creditors.

But investors have the strongest interest in the earnings performance of the business. They use certain key ratios to evaluate its profit track record.

This chapter briefly explains the basic financial statement ratios used by creditors and investors. These ratios are the basic "scores" by which managers are judged by the suppliers of capital to the business.

EXHIBIT M—THE COMPANY'S FINANCIAL STATEMENTS FOR ITS FIRST YEAR
(Modified Slightly to Show Total Liabilities)

BALANCE SHEET AT END OF YEAR

Current Assets			Current Liabilities		
Cash		$ 243,000	Accounts Payable		$ 269,120
Accounts Receivable		405,000	Accrued Expenses		130,390
Inventory		632,400	Income Tax Payable		10,200
Prepaid Expenses		77,760	Short-Term Notes Payable		300,000
Total Current Assets		$1,358,160	Total Current Liabilities		$ 709,710
			Long-Term Notes Payable		525,000
			Total Liabilities		$1,234,710
Property, Plant & Equipment			Stockholders' Equity		
Land, Building, Machines,			Capital Stock	$766,030	
Equipment, and Furniture	$918,800		Retained Earnings	198,000	$ 964,030
Accumulated Depreciation	(78,220)	$ 840,580			
Total Assets		$2,198,740	Total Liabilities & Stockholders' Equity		$2,198,740

The financial statements of the same company analyzed in the early chapters serve as the example in this chapter again. For convenience the company's Balance Sheet at the end of its first year of business and its Income Statement for the year are reproduced here—see Exhibit M, which we'll refer to often in this chapter.

Notice that the Cash Flow Statement for the year is not repeated. None of the ratios discussed in this chapter involve this statement, which may come as a surprise to you. Why not? Two reasons seem to explain this. First, the statement is designed to read as a whole and is limited to the sources and uses of cash during the year. Cash flow is vital, but not the complete story about the business.

Second, until recently the Cash Flow Statement has not been included in external financial reports, so creditors and investors did not have this information readily available. There are virtually no standard or benchmark ratios for cash flow. Perhaps some cash flow ratios will emerge now that the Cash Flow Statement is required in financial reports.

INCOME STATEMENT FOR FIRST YEAR

Sales Revenue		$4,212,000
Cost of Goods Sold Expense		2,740,400
Gross Margin		$1,471,600
Operating Expenses	$1,010,880	
Depreciation Expense	78,220	1,089,100
Operating Earnings		$ 382,500
Interest Expense		82,500
Earnings Before Income Tax		$ 300,000
Income Tax Expense		102,000
Net Income		$ 198,000

Debt-Paying Ability (Solvency) Ratios

Always a key question is whether a business will be able to pay its liabilities when they come due. Failure to pay its debt on time damages the credit rating of the business, of course, and may jeopardize its very existence if the unpaid creditors take legal action to enforce collection. The sharp rise in business failures, including the bankruptcies of many well-known corporations during the recession of the early 1980s, underscores the importance of keeping a close watch on the debt-paying ability of a business.

The Current Ratio: The Basic Test of Short-Term Solvency

One "classic" and widely used ratio to test the short-term debt-paying ability of a company is its *current ratio*, which is the company's total current assets divided by its total current liabilities. From the data in Exhibit M, the current ratio for the company is computed as follows:

$$\text{Current Ratio} = \frac{\text{Total Current Assets}}{\text{Total Current Liabilities}} = \frac{\$1,358,160}{\$709,710} = 1.91$$

The current ratio may be expressed as 1.91 to 1.00, but hardly ever as a percent (191%).

The general rule of thumb is that the current ratio should be 2 to 1 or higher. Most businesses find that a minimum 2 to 1 current ratio is applied by their creditors. In other words, short-term creditors generally limit the credit extended a business to ½ or less of the company's short-term assets. Given this credit limit, a company's current assets will be twice or more its current liabilities.

Why do short-term creditors put such a limit on a business? One reason is to provide a safety cushion. A current ratio of 2 to 1 means there is $2 of cash or assets that will be converted into cash during the near future available to pay each dollar of current liabilities (which come due in the near future). Each dollar of short-term debt is "backed up" with two dollars of present cash or future near-term cash inflow. The "extra" dollar of current assets provides a nice margin of safety.

Theoretically, a company could remain solvent with a 1 to 1 current ratio. The three noninterest-bearing liabilities—Accounts Payable, Accrued Expenses, and Income Tax Payable—supply total credit equal to, say, about ⅓ of total current assets. With this base of current liabilities, the company could conceivably convince bankers or other lenders to make short-term loans for the other ⅔ of current assets. But this would leave no safety margin for the lenders. Few, if any, short-term lenders would go this far out on a limb.

After all, creditors are not owners—they don't share in the net income earned by the business. The income on their loans is limited to the interest rates they charge. As a creditor they quite properly minimize their loan risks; as limited-income investors, they must.

In short, suppliers of short-term loans to business decide what the minimum current ratio will be, and usually they do not allow it to drop below 2 to 1.

However, the 2 to 1 minimum is only a rule of thumb; there are exceptions. Some companies such as car dealers can borrow almost 100% on their inventories, so their current liabilities are more than ½ their current assets. Before accepting the 2 for 1 ratio for a business, it is a good idea to check the *average* current ratio for companies in the industry. For example, Dun & Bradstreet publishes the current ratio for a large number of industries. Motor vehicle dealers, as just mentioned, traditionally have carried on business with a 1.5 to 1.0 current ratio.

The Acid Test Ratio (or Quick Ratio)

Inventory is many weeks away from conversion into cash. Products are held 2, 3, or 4 months before sale. If the sale is made on credit, which is normal, there's another waiting period before the receivables are collected. In short, inventory is not nearly as liquid as Accounts Receivable; it takes a lot longer to convert Inventory into cash.

The *acid test ratio* excludes Inventory (and Prepaid Expenses also). The total of Cash, Marketable Securities (if any), and Accounts Receivable is divided by total current liabilities to compute the acid test ratio. It is also called the *quick ratio* because only cash and assets quickly convertible into cash are included in the ratio. In this example the company's acid test ratio is computed as follows:

$$\text{Acid Test Ratio} = \frac{\text{Cash} + \text{Accounts Receivable}}{\text{Total Current Liabilities}}$$

$$= \frac{\$243,000 + \$405,000}{\$709,710} = .91$$

The rule of thumb is that the acid test ratio should be 1 to 1 or higher, although you find many more exceptions to this rule of thumb than the 2 to 1 current ratio.

Debt to Equity Ratio

Some debt is good, but too much debt is dangerous. The debt to equity ratio is an indicator whether a company is using debt to its advantage, or perhaps going too far and is overburdened with debt.

For the company in this example (see Exhibit M), the debt to equity ratio is computed as follows:

$$\frac{\text{Debt/Equity}}{\text{Ratio}} = \frac{\text{Total Liabilities}}{\text{Total Stockholders' Equity}} = \frac{\$1,234,710}{\$964,030} = 1.28$$

In brief, the company is using $1.28 of liabilities for every $1.00 of owners' (stockholders') equity in the business. Notice that *all* liabilities (noninterest as well as interest bearing, and both short-term and long-term) are included, and *all* stockholders' equity (paid-in capital plus retained earnings) is included in the debt to equity ratio.

This business, at a 1.28 to 1.00 debt to equity ratio, would be viewed as moderately leveraged. The company is taking fairly aggressive advantage of debt capital relative to its base of equity capital. Most businesses stay below a 1 to 1 debt to equity ratio, because they don't want to take on so much debt or because they can't convince creditors to loan them more than one-half of their assets. However, some industries are exceptions to this rule of thumb, and traditionally have had debt to equity ratios more than 1 to 1, much higher in some lines of business and for financial institutions in particular.

Return on Investment Ratios: How Financial Leverage Helps (Usually)

Stock investors take the risk of whether the business can earn a profit and sustain its profit performance over the years. The value of their stock depends first and foremost on the profit-making record and potential of the business.

The basic test of a company's profit performance for its stockholders is not simply how much profit it earns, but rather how much profit is earned relative to how much stockholders' equity (capital) is being used to earn that profit. $100,000 annual net income relative to $250,000 stockholders' capital base is very good. $100,000 annual net income relative to $2,500,000 stockholders' capital base is very poor.

Dividing annual net income by total stockholders' equity gives the *return on equity* (*ROE*) ratio; for this company it is computed as follows:

$$\text{Return on Equity} = \frac{\text{Net Income}}{\text{Total Stockholders' Equity}} = \frac{\$198,000}{\$964,030} = 20.54\%$$

By most standards a 20.54% ROE would be judged pretty good. But, again, the ROE should be compared with industry-wide averages for the current year to get a true reading.

ROE is the bottom-line return on investment (ROI) ratio for stockholders. Bottom-line profit (net income) is divided by the stockholders' equity in the business. Other ROI ratios are also useful in analyzing a company's profit performance.

Another very important ROI ratio for profit analysis is the *return on assets* (ROA) ratio. The *before-tax* ROA ratio is Operating Earnings (before interest and income tax) divided by Total Assets; for this company it is computed as follows:

$$\text{Before-Tax Return on Assets} = \frac{\text{Operating Earnings Before Interest and Income Tax}}{\text{Total Assets}}$$

$$= \frac{\$382,500}{\$2,198,740} = 17.40\%$$

The before-tax ROA ratio tells us that the company earned more than 17¢ profit before interest and income tax on each dollar of assets used in the business.

The before-tax ROA is compared with the annual interest rate on borrowed funds. In this example the company's annual interest rate on its short-term and long-term debt is 10.00%.

The company can earn 17.40% on the money borrowed. So there is a favorable "spread" of 7.40% between the two. This difference between the two rates is the nub of *financial leverage*. Financial leverage means using debt capital on which a business can earn a higher before-tax ROA than the annual interest rate paid on the debt.

The total benefit from financial leverage can be computed fairly simply for a business. In this example the company has interest-bearing debt, as well as current liabilities on which no interest is paid. (This is true for almost all businesses, of course.) In total, all its liabilities supply $1,234,710 of the company's total assets (see Exhibit M on page 142).

The total cost for the use of this capital is the $82,500 interest expense for the year. Thus the company makes a sizable financial leverage gain on its liabilities, which is computed as follows:

Financial Leverage Gain for the Year

$1,234,710	×	17.40%	=	$214,840	(Operating earnings before interest and income tax that is earned on the capital supplied by liabilities)
(Total Liabilities)		(Before-Tax ROA)			
				−82,500	(Interest expense)
				$132,340	(Financial leverage gain for year)

Financial leverage provided over $132,000 of the $382,500 earnings before income tax for the year, or about 35%.

In a poor year a company's before-tax ROA may be less than its annual interest rate. In this situation financial leverage (on borrowed funds) works against the company. The high interest rates of the early 1980s combined with the severe slippage in before-tax ROA suffered by many businesses during this recessionary period provide ample proof of this point. The use of debt only aggravated an already bad situation for many corporations. Financial leverage cuts both ways, it should be remembered.

Price/Earnings (P/E) Ratio

The stock shares of more than ten thousand corporations are traded in public markets such as the New York Stock Exchange. The day-to-day market value of these shares receives a great deal of attention, to say the least. Market value, more than anything else, depends on the earnings ability of the corporation. Therefore, market value is compared to net income (earnings after interest and income tax, or the final, bottom-line earnings of the corporation).

Because market value is per share, net income (earnings) has to be put on a per share basis. The basic idea of computing *earnings per share* (EPS) can be put as follows:

$$\text{Earnings per Share (EPS)} = \frac{\text{Net Income for Year}}{\substack{\text{Total Number of Stock Shares} \\ \text{Participating in Net Income}}}$$

EPS is not simple to compute, despite the relative simplicity of the concept. Many corporations use fairly complicated stock structures. They may issue preferred stock shares in addition to common stock shares. Their debt (and preferred stock) securities may be convertible into their common stock shares. Many other conditions affect the computation of the EPS.

In any case, once EPS is computed it is compared with the market price of the stock. The *price/earnings (P/E) ratio* is computed as follows:

$$\text{Price/Earnings (P/E) Ratio} = \frac{\text{Current Market Price}}{\text{Earnings per Share}}$$

Suppose the stock shares were trading at $24.00 per share, and the corporation's EPS for the most recent year is $3.00. Thus its P/E ratio is 8.00. Like all the other ratios discussed in this chapter, the P/E ratio has to be compared against industry-wide and marketwide averages to tell if it's too high or too low. Much depends on how stock investors forecast the future earnings prospects of the corporation.

The P/E ratio is so important that the *Wall Street Journal* includes it with other market trading information for all common stock shares reported in the New York Stock Exchange (NYSE)—Composite Transactions as well as the American Stock Exchange (Amex)—Composite Transactions.

The P/E ratio does not apply to private corporations, whose stock shares are not traded. The stock owners and managers of these companies judge profit (earnings) performance mainly by Return on Equity (ROE) and other return on investment ratios. One of their main concerns is how to maintain and improve ROE.

Last, it should be mentioned that EPS must be reported in the Income Statements of publicly owned corporations. This reporting requirement also provides evidence of just how important EPS is. In contrast, none of the other ratios discussed in this chapter *have to* be reported, although many companies do report their current ratios and return on asset and equity ratios.

Return on Equity: Final Comments

How can a business improve a poor ROE, or maintain a good ROE? Three factors are key:

1. Financial leverage—keep the debt to equity ratio at the optimum level.

2. Sales revenue on assets—keep the sales to assets ratio as high as possible.

3. Control expenses—keep the expense to sales ratio as low as possible.

In brief, use debt to best advantage, make the best sales revenue use of assets, and keep expenses as low as possible. Each of these three key factors is discussed in turn.

The company in this example is already at a debt to equity ratio of 1.28 (see page 145). As a practical matter the company probably couldn't increase this ratio very much. So not much improvement in its ROE can be made here.

Profit derives from sales. The higher the sales revenue from a particular set (given mix) of assets the better, unless the company sells at a loss. In this case the company's annual sales revenue is $4,212,000 compared with $2,198,740 total assets (see Exhibit M). Sales are just under two times assets; this key relationship is measured in the *asset turnover ratio*, which is computed as follows:

$$\text{Asset Turnover Ratio} = \frac{\text{Sales Revenue}}{\text{Total Assets}} = \frac{\$4,212,000}{\$2,198,740} = 1.91$$

If the company could squeeze out more sales from the same assets, its profit and thus its ROE should increase. The additional sales revenue should normally yield additional profit. Put in reverse, a decrease in the Asset Turnover Ratio will decrease the ROE.

Last, profit can be improved by reducing the ratio of expenses to sales revenue. Certainly every business should be cost conscious and continuously be on a program of cost containment and reduction. Its managers should ruthlessly examine every dollar of expense. The Internal Revenue Service, of all people, probably has the best approach. The IRS demands two tests for any expense to be deductible—the expense must be *necessary* and must be *reasonable* in amount. It's hard to think of better guidelines for business managers.

24

A FEW PARTING COMMENTS

A few years ago a local Woman's Investment Club invited me to their monthly meeting to discuss the meaning and uses of financial statements. It was a lot of fun, and it also forced me to rethink a few basic points. A fairly sophisticated group, these ladies pool their monthly contributions and invest mainly in common stocks. Several of their questions were incisive, although one point caught me by surprise.

As I recall, at that time they were thinking of buying 100 common stock shares in General Electric. Two members presented their research on the company and recommended buying the stock at the going market price. The discussion caused me to suspect that several thought their money would go to GE for use in its business. I pointed out that, no, the money would go to the seller of the shares, not to GE.

They were not clear on the fundamental difference between the *primary capital market* (the original, first-time issue of securities by corporations for money that flows directly into the coffers of the business) and the *secondary capital market* (in which present owners sell their securities to other investors, with no money going to the corporations who issued the securities). I compared this difference with the purchase of a new car in which money goes to GM, Ford, or Chrysler (through the dealer) versus the purchase of a *used* car in which the money goes to the previous owner.

We cleared up that point, though I think they were disappointed that GE wouldn't get their money. The distinction between the two capital markets also made them realize that while they were of the opinion that the going market value was a good price to buy at, the party on the other side of the trade must think it was a good price to *sell* at.

On other matters they asked very good questions. I'd like to share some of these with you in this chapter and offer a few other important points for individuals investing in corporate stock and debt securities. These questions are also important when buying a business *as a whole*—for corporate raiders attempting hostile takeovers; corporate managers engineering a leveraged buyout of the business; one corporation taking over another; or, purchasing a closely held business. Buyouts and takeovers bring up the business valuation question, which also is discussed briefly.

Some Basic Questions and Answers

Investors in corporate stock and debt securities should know the answers to the following fundamental questions concerning financial statements. These questions are answered from the viewpoint of the typical individual investor—not institutional investors, professional investment managers, or security analysts. My pension fund holds over $60 billion of investments. I assume its investment professionals already know the answers to these questions. They'd better!

Are financial statements reliable and trustworthy?

Yes, the vast majority of audited financial statements are presented fairly according to established reporting standards, which are called generally accepted accounting principles (GAAP). If not, the CPA auditor will call deviations or shortcomings to your attention. So, be sure to read the auditor's report. You should realize, however, that GAAP are not static. Over time these fundamental financial reporting standards and guidelines change and evolve.

Accounting's rule-making authorities constantly monitor financial reporting practices and problem areas. They make changes when needed, to keep abreast of changes in business and financial practices, as well as developments in the broader political, legal, and economic world that business operates in.

Nevertheless, are some financial statements misleading and fraudulent?

Yes, unfortunately. *The Wall Street Journal* carries many stories of high-level management fraud—illegal payments, misuse of assets, and known losses were concealed; expenses were underrecorded; sales revenues were overrecorded or sales returns were not recorded; and, financial distress symptoms were buried out of sight.

It is very difficult for CPA auditors to catch high-level management fraud that has been cleverly concealed or that involves a conspiracy among managers and other parties to the fraud. Auditors are highly skilled professionals, and the rate of audit failures has been very low. Sometimes, however, the auditors were lax in their duties and deserved to be sued—and were. Now and then CPA firms have had to pay out millions of dollars to defrauded investors.

There's always a small risk that the financial statements are, in fact, false or seriously misleading. You would have legal recourse against the company's managers and its auditors once the fraud is found out, but this is not a happy situation. Almost certainly you'd still end up losing money, even after recovering some of your losses through legal action.

Is it worth your time as an individual investor to read carefully through the financial statements and also to compute ratios and make other interpretations?

No, not really. The Woman's Investment Club was very surprised by this answer, and I don't blame them. The conventional wisdom is that by diligent reading of financial statements you will discover under- or overvalued securities. But, the evidence doesn't support this assumption. Market prices reflect all publicly available information about a business, including the information in its latest quarterly and annual financial reports.

If you enjoy reading through financial statements, as I do, fine. It's a valuable learning experience. But don't expect to find out something that the market doesn't already know. It's very unlikely that you might find a nugget of information that has been overlooked by everyone else. Forget it; it's not worth your time as an investor. The same time would be better spent keeping up with current developments reported in the financial press.

Why should you read financial statements, then?

To know what you are getting into, I would answer. Does the company have a lot of debt and a heavy interest load to carry? For that matter, is the company in bankruptcy or in a workout situation? Has the company had a consistent earnings record over the last 5 to 10 years, or has its profit ridden a roller coaster over this time? Has the company consistently paid a cash dividend for many years? Has the company issued more than one class of stock? Which stock are you buying, relative to any other classes?

You would obviously inspect a house before getting serious about buying it, to see if it has two stories, three or more bedrooms, a basement, its general appearance, and so on. Likewise, you should know the "financial architecture" of a business before putting your capital in its securities. Financial statements serve this getting acquainted purpose very well.

One basic stock investment strategy is to search through financial reports or financial statement information stored in computer data bases, to find corporations that meet certain criteria—for example, whose market values are less than their book values, or whose cash plus cash equivalents per share is more than a certain percent of current market value. Whether or not these stocks end up outperforming the market is another question. In any case, financial statements can be culled through to find whatever types of corporations you are looking for.

Is there any one "litmus test" for a quick test on a company's financial statements?

Yes. I would suggest that you compute the percent increase (or decrease) in sales revenue this year over last year, and use this percent as the baseline for testing changes in bottom-line profit (net income) and major assets. Assume sales revenue increased 10% over last year. Did profit increase 10%? Did Accounts Receivable and Inventory increase 10%?

This is no more than a "quick and dirty" method, but it will point out major disparities. For instance, suppose Inventory jumped 50% even though sales revenue increased only 10%. This may signal a major management mistake; the overstock of inventory might lead to write-downs later. Management does *not* usually comment on such disparities in their financial reports. You'll have to find them yourself.

Do conservative accounting methods cause conservative market values?

It doesn't seem so. Every business must make difficult accounting choices from the menu of generally accepted alternatives. Roughly half select conservative accounting methods to measure profit (net income), which also results in conservative book values for their assets and liabilities. Note, however, that conservative accounting methods might in a particular year cause opposite effects, i.e., higher earnings, because of such things as LIFO liquidation gains in that year.

The evidence suggests that the securities market as a whole takes differences in profit measurement methods into account in determining stock market values. In other words, "the market is not fooled" by differences in accounting methods—even though earnings, assets, and liabilities are reported on different bases of accounting from company to company. To be honest,

this is not an easy conclusion to prove. But, overall, differences in accounting methods seem to be adjusted for in the marketplace. For instance, a company cannot simply switch its accounting methods to improve the market price of its stock shares. The market does not behave this way.

Do financial statements report the truth, the whole truth, and nothing but the truth?

On the one hand, disclosure in financial reports is fair and not misleading. On the other hand, the general pattern of financial report disclosure is not as complete and frank as it could be and ought to be. The large majority of companies are reluctant to lay bare "all the facts." And, bad news is suppressed or de-emphasized as long as possible. Clearly, there is a lack of candor and open discussion in financial reports. Few companies are willing to wash their dirty linen in public by making full disclosure in their financial reports.

There is a management analysis and discussion section in financial reports, but usually it is a fairly "sanitized" version of what happened during the year. The history of financial reporting disclosure practices, unfortunately, makes clear that until standard-setting authorities force specific disclosure standards on all companies, few make such disclosures voluntarily.

The disclosure of employee pension and retirement costs went through this pattern of inadequate reporting until, finally, the standard-setting bodies stepped in and required fuller disclosure. Until a standard was recently issued, most companies were reluctant to report a Cash Flow Statement even though this statement had been asked for by security analysts since the 1950s!

Recalls of unsafe products, pending lawsuits, and top management compensation are other examples of reluctant reporting. The masthead of the *New York Times* boasts "All the News That's Fit to Print." Don't expect this in financial reports, however.

Do financial statements explain the basic profit-making strategy of the business?

Not really. In an ideal world, I would argue, a financial report should provide a profit roadmap or an earnings blueprint of the business. The financial report reader should be told the basic profit-making strategy of the business, including the key success factors at the core of its profit making. But, this is not found in financial reports. The best an investor can do is to go to other sources.

For example, an article in the *Wall Street Journal* on General Motors's 1988 profit performance pointed out that total rebates to its car buyers for the year were about equal to its entire net income for the year. However, this rather important point is not discussed in GM's 1988 annual financial report. Indeed, the word "rebate" is avoided like the plague in GM's annual report.

In their annual financial reports publicly owned corporations are required to include a breakdown of their total sales revenue and operating expenses by major segments (lines of business), which provides information about which parts of the business are more profitable than others. For example, a large part of GM's 1988 profit came from its overseas operations. However,

segment data are very large, conglomerate totals that span many different products. Businesses do not report profit margins of their key products. Security analysts focus much attention on profit margins, but you don't find this information in financial reports. And, you don't find any separation between *fixed* as opposed to *variable* expenses in Income Statements, which is essential for profit analysis.

If you were to study managerial accounting, you'd quickly learn that the first step is to go back to square one and recast the Income Statement into a management planning and decision-making structure, one that focuses on profit margins and cost behavior. [Without undue modesty I can recommend a book I wrote on this subject.*] In short, the Income Statement in an external financial report is far different from what you would see if you were the president of the business, and I don't mean the level of detail but rather the general profit-making scheme of the business.

Does its Balance Sheet report the worth of a business?

No. A Balance Sheet does not pretend to report what the value of a business would be on the auction block. Until there's a serious buyer or an actual takeover attempt it's anyone's guess how much a business would fetch. The book value of Owner's Equity reported in a company's Balance Sheet is not a good indicator of what the business might sell for. The value of a business depends mainly on its profit-making history and

---

* *Profit Dynamics: Achieving Consistent Bottom Line Results*, John A. Tracy, Dow Jones-Irwin (Homewood, Illinois), 1989.

prospects and only secondarily on its assets and liabilities—although every case is different.

A business might have valuable assets that the buyer wants for the purpose of selling them off, or the buyer may be planning radical changes in the financial structure of the business. For these reasons, and others, the value paid for a business often differs dramatically from the book value of its Owners' Equity. There have been cases of a buyer paying less than the total of a company's cash and cash equivalents (minus its liabilities). In other words, the buyer bought in for less than the immediate liquidation value of the business. But this is rare.

Financial statements, as you see them, are prepared on the *going concern* basis, not on a *business valuation* basis. Business value is relevant in an actual buyout situation of course, and when a value has to be put on a privately owned business for estate tax purposes. Otherwise, there is no pressing reason to go to the time and cost of estimating the current replacement values of a company's assets and the current settlement values of its liabilities. What would be the point? Therefore, Owners' Equity (being assets minus liabilities) is not based on current values, but rather is based on the historical book values of the company's assets and liabilities.

Current values usually are close to book values for certain assets—Cash, Marketable Securities Investments, Accounts Receivable, and FIFO-based Inventory, for example. On the other hand, the book value of LIFO-based Inventory and the book values of fixed assets depreciated by accelerated methods may be far below their current replacement values. Land is another such example.

But to repeat an earlier point: the value of a business typically depends on its profit-making ability as projected into the future. A buyer may be willing to pay 10 or more times the annual net income of a closely owned, private business. Likewise, investors keep a close eye on the price/earnings (P/E) ratios of stocks issued by publicly owned corporations. Seldom does a stock's market value hinge directly on the corporation's Balance Sheet, unless financial disaster is looming in the immediate future and investors are of the opinion that the liquidation of the business is a real threat.

A Short Summary

You can rely on audited financial statements; the risk of fraudulent financial reports is minimal. Think twice before analyzing the financial statements of publicly traded corporate securities; it isn't worth your time. On the other hand, for a quick benchmark test compare the percent change in the company's sales revenue with the percent changes in its earnings and major assets. Major disparities are worth a look.

Reading financial statements is the best way of getting acquainted with the financial structure of a business you're thinking of investing in. Don't worry about whether the business uses conservative accounting methods; there seems to be no adverse effect on the market values of their stock shares.

Financial disclosure practices leave a lot to be desired. And, don't look for the profit strategy of a business to be explained in its financial statements. Last, the total value of a business is not found in its Balance Sheet. Its value depends primarily on the assessment of its profit-making ability in the past and for the future.

This last chapter may seem to have a somewhat negative tone. This is not my intent at all. Rather, the main message is to be cautious in making decisions based on financial statements. Many investors and managers don't seem fully aware of the limitations of financial statements. Used intelligently, financial statements are the indispensable starting point for management and investment decisions. I hope the book helps you make better decisions. Good luck!

INDEX